SEMIOTEXT(E) INTERVENTION SERIES

© 2010 Semiotext(e) and Jean Baudrillard
This translation © 2010 by Semiotext(e)

Published by Semiotext(e)
2007 Wilshire Blvd., Suite 427, Los Angeles, CA 90057
www.semiotexte.com

Thanks to Marine Baudrillard, Marc Lowenthal and John Ebert.

Inside cover photograph: Jean Baudrillard
Design: Hedi El Kholti

ISBN: 978-1-58435-092-7
Distributed by The MIT Press, Cambridge, Mass.
and London, England
Printed in the United States of America

10 9 8 7 6 5 4

Jean Baudrillard

The Agony of Power

Introduction by Sylvère Lotringer

Translated by Ames Hodges

semiotext(e)
intervention
series □ 6

Contents

Introduction by Sylvère Lotringer   7

From Domination to Hegemony   33

The White Terror of World Order   59

Where Good Grows   79

The Roots of Evil   109

Introduction

DOMINATION AND SERVITUDE

This book gathers previously unpublished texts written in 2005, two years before the author's death. Jean Baudrillard read them at various conferences around the world, in Rio de Janeiro, Montreal, New York, Quito, etc. By then, he had become an itinerant philosopher—he never was much of a "home" philosopher anyway. I joined him in Montreal in late October 2005, where he delivered the first text included here, "From Domination to Hegemony." He was taking a crack at the bewildering situation currently facing us as we exit the system of "domination" (based on slavery, obedience, alienation) and enter a more expansive world of "hegemony," in which everyone becomes both hostage and accomplice of the global power. It was a very powerful text, and I offered to publish it right away in English. Baudrillard was hoping to turn all the texts he was writing at the time into a new book, so I held off.

A few months later he was diagnosed with cancer and never regained enough strength to follow up on this project. I am publishing these texts, slightly edited to avoid duplication, into a book in order to fulfill, at least partially, his wishes.[1] I simply added an interview that he gave that same year to *Chronic'art*, a French cultural magazine, which he reviewed personally. Baudrillard wasn't one to make a final statement—he didn't take himself that seriously—but this book could certainly be read as his intellectual testament. Only a free mind could have written it. Like Nietzsche, Baudrillard never was afraid of shaking everything that was already crumbling down, whatever the outcome.

Leaving Montreal, we came back to New York where we had scheduled a public dialogue between ourselves at the New School for Social Research in early November. It took place in front of a packed audience, and hundreds more people lined up good-humoredly in the street. It was Baudrillard's last trip to the United States, and it turned into a festival. Everyone wanted to check for themselves whether Baudrillard was for real or a simulacrum of himself. And here he was at the center of the huge empty stage—a stocky, soft-spoken bespectacled little man with a large Native-American face, mumbling some

---

1. Two other texts were published separately as *Carnival and Cannibal*, trans. Chris Turner, London, Seagull Books, 2010.

English with a German-sounding accent. I am not sure anyone understood everything that was said, but the audience was ecstatic. It was philosophy by contact. This is the way theory was being accomodated in an age of media spectacle. But why should theory be spared the general decomposition of all values, which is turning culture, politics, not to mention life itself, into a carnival? Even Slavoj Žižek slavishly said of Alain Badiou, playing each other up, that he was "Plato walking among us." Why not Mao himself? As Baudrillard wrote: "History that repeats itself turns to farce. But a farce that repeats itself ends up making a history." The event was history.

Very early on, Baudrillard mapped out most of the concepts that he would work on for decades to come. As he recognized it himself, a philosopher may only have *one* idea in his life, and be lucky that he has one, but he could unfold it in such a way that no one would recognize it whenever they passed by it again. Actually, Baudrillard had two major ideas: the first one, critical, was that reality has disappeared and was replaced by simulacra; the second one, more agonistic, was to turn this disappearance into a symbolic challenge.

The agonistic challenge was what he really cared about, but simulation and simulacra is what people remembered him for most, often taking it, erroneously, as an advocation on his part. It was in fact a *jubilant* diagnosis of our civilization. Baudrillard could never quite believe his eyes when faced with what we keep doing to ourselves in the name of—whatever. Like Antonin Artaud, Baudrillard realized from the onset that our culture was getting divorced from life. By the time he was writing, there was not much life left to be divorced from. Baudrillard was hailed as the inventor of "post-modernism," a concept he rejected. The same confusion surrounded Michel Foucault, who was cast as the stern advocate of control, or Paul Virilio cast as the prophet of speed. The publication of *Simulations* gave Baudrillard instant prominence in the New York art world. It got him pigeonholed as the denier of reality, and he was adulated or hated for it. He was in fact already working on other concepts—seduction, fatality, ecstasy—by the time simulation became the rage. "Simulation" never was Baudrillard's signature concept, the way the "society of the spectacle" was for Guy Debord, although the two notions remain closely related. Simulation is spectacle without an agency. The concept got out of hand, the way the Oedipus Complex did for Freud, who only wrote eight pages all in all about it. The two parts that make up *Simulations* were only put together in the book I published in English in the Foreign Agents series in 1983. In French, they belong to different books. "Simulation" was first mentioned in *The Consumer*

Society—published in 1970, a couple of years after Debord's *Society of the Spectacle*. Fittingly, Baudrillard managed to turn Ferdinand de Saussure's discovery of linguistic *value* (signs as pure differences) into a "structural revolution." It was a clinical assessment of a society that was losing all its moorings. Identifying the code independently of any outside reference allowed him to read the sign on the wall— the floatation of value escaping into boundless speculation. Politics after that could never be the same.

The major turn in Baudrillard's thinking, paradoxically, happened in America. An invitation by Marxist Fredric Jameson to teach for a few months in San Diego in 1975, together with Jean-François Lyotard, Michel de Certeau, Louis Marin and Edgar Morin, turned out to be decisive. The two camps didn't always see eye to eye, and there were occasional tensions and mutual exclusions, which I happened to witness at the time, but it certainly was a learning process on both sides, and had lasting repercussions. Baudrillard took a huge step forward when he discovered the "Silicon Valley" phenomenon, the home-based computer utopia, which he hailed as the "cybernetic disintegration of the 'tertiary metropolis.'"[2] [45] Until

---

2. Jean Baudrillard, *Symbolic Exchange and Death*, trans. Iain Hamilton Grant, London, Sage Publications, 1993, p. 45. All the page numbers in this introduction refer to this book.

then, he had seen the sphere of consumption as a mere appendage of the sphere of production, the way superstructures sat on infrastructures in Marxist theory. Registering the California effect, Baudrillard realized that production was moving into consumption. His analysis of the consumer society hadn't been a limited case study; it applied *everywhere*. The consumer process couldn't be stopped, it would engulf everything. Soon, the entire world would be "consumed" by the exchangeability of capital. "Everything within production and the economy becomes commutable, reversible and exchangeable according to the same indeterminate specularity as we find in politics, fashion or the media." [16] Capital no longer was a process of production; production itself was dissolving into the code. [18] He also understood that there was no more gap left, no insider's distance that would still allow for a critique of society. Any counter-discourse filtering into the code would immediately be "disconnected from its own ends, disintegrated and absorbed" like everything else. [2]

Before leaving San Diego, Baurillard feverishly completed his *magnum opus, Symbolic Exchange and Death*, which he published the following year, a thick and rambling book that served as a scaffolding for everything that he would try out in the

years to come. While Deleuze and Guattari maintained that society keeps leaking from all sides and
that capital never stops investing and disinvesting
territories with its flows, Baudrillard's own version
of capital, the structural revolution of value, was
anything but fluid. On the contrary, it was a
homogenizing principle based on repetition,
bringing together differences from various sources
on a larger and larger scale. By an "extraordinary
coincidence," Baudrillard recalled, he had turned
to Freud just at the moment when he realized that
the system of production was moving to the
sphere of reproduction. It dawned on him that the
entire political economy was governed by the
death drive. [148] In its most "terroristic structural
form," the law of value was a "compulsive reproduction of the code." It was death on the march,
and "the destiny of our culture." [152]

The death drive keeps unbinding energy and
returning it to a prior, inorganic state. Freud treated
it as a biological metaphor, but also as a myth,
"magnificent in its indefiniteness." Using Freud
against Freud, Baudrillard celebrated it as an
amazing breakthrough, a major *anthropological*
discovery. This sent him back, via Mauss and
Bataille, to ancient cults and primitive formations.
Although he would hardly refer to it by name, the
death drive became the keystone of his entire
work. The exaltation that he felt then, seeing

everything suddenly coming together, reverberates through *Symbolic Exchange and Death*, especially in the preface, which takes on a visionary quality: "Everywhere, in every domain, a single form predominates: reversibility, cyclical reversal and annulment put an end to the linearity of time, language, economic exchange, accumulation and power. Hence the reversibility of the gift in the counter-gift, the reversibility of exchange in the sacrifice, the reversibility of time in the cycle... In every domain it assumes the form of extermination and death, for it is the form of the symbolic itself." [2] Reversibility is the form death takes in a symbolic exchange. And Baudrillard warned Deleuze and Guattari that "all the freed energies will one day return to it... For the system is the master: like God it can bind or unbind energies; what it is incapable of (and what it can no longer avoid) is reversibility." [5]

At the time Baudrillard was witnessing the twilight of labor culture in the deserts of California, the Operaist movement in Italy was experimenting with the same idea, but on a much larger scale, voluntarily renouncing steady employment and relying instead on collective intelligence and technological advances. Italian autonomists saw themselves as a new breed of communists, and yet they were open-ended enough to look to America for innovative forms of labor and freer trade-unionism along the line of the Wobblies (the International Workers of the World) who had organized immigrant workers in the 1920s. Félix Guattari publicly espoused their cause in France, Toni Negri conceived it in Italy, and Jean Baudrillard dreamed it in America. They all had reached the same conclusions: the Fordist system, with communist parties and labor bureaucracy locked together, was blocking any change. It had to be replaced by "zero work" and "cottage industries."

Compared to the French "Glorious Three," 1830, 1848 and the 1871 Paris Commune, May '68 was a failed revolution, but it succeeded in other ways. It demonstrated that traditional class struggle no longer was a viable political alternative. The "revolutionaries" remained on the sideline, and the rebels were already engaged in repro-duction. Italian autonomists saw the coming Postfordist paradigm as radical utopia, it was the "communism of capital."[3] Baudrillard wasn't so sure. Looking at it as part of the "revolution of value," he realized that Postfordism and the new technologies of labor could well be another step towards an "integral reality" that no one would be

---

3. Paolo Virno, *Grammar of the Multitude*, trans. Isabella Bertoletti, James Cascaito, and Andrea Casson, Los Angeles, Semiotext(e), 2003, p. 110.

able to oppose, short of capitalism itself. The intellectual split became unavoidable. In the 1980s, the "winter years," Baudrillard's extrapolations were rejected by his peers as "weak thought."

The consequences of the paradigmatic change indeed were huge, and they could be read in different ways. Immaterializing labor allowed the form of capital to penetrate the entire society. It invested workers both at home and in the social space "as one might 'invest' a town, totally occupying it and controlling all access." [19]. No longer brutally bought and sold on the marketplace, labor power became another commodity. Labor and non-labor time (exchange value and use value) became harder to differentiate, as Baudrillard had anticipated, and the extraction of surplus-value problematic. The passage from the golden age of production to the *social factory* was exciting; for some, like Toni Negri and Paolo Virno, it promised the deployment of a "general intelligence" open to change and innovation. Looking at it the other way, it was nonstop work and general stupidity. The structure of absorption became total. Pulverized "into every pore of society," labor became *a way of life*. In 1976, the year Baudrillard published *Symbolic Exchange*, Foucault introduced the concept of "bio-power" in his lectures at the College de France. Their confrontation in *Forget Foucault*, one year later, could be read again in that light. It may well have been a missed encounter.

Like Foucault, Baudrillard had been deeply affected by the work of Antonin Artaud and Georges Bataille, "high modernists" who introduced them both to Nietzsche, but their influence on Baudrillard remained long-lasting. Both Artaud's "theater of cruelty" and Bataille's "sacrifices" were attempts to recreate a symbolic bond in a world increasingly estranged from it. The concept of "cruelty," inspired by Nietzsche, involved strict rules that had to be applied with an implacable rigor. The display of gruesome tortures and dismemberments in Foucault's *Discipline and Punish*, published the same year, were cruel in that way: the ritual of power was meant to inflict on the regicide's body pains that would be, down to the last detail, commensurate to the outrage.

In the classical—legal—conception of sovereignty, the monarch isn't just considered superior ("sovereign") to his miserable subjects in relative terms. Ruling by divine right, his superiority is absolute and transcends vulgar human existence. *Taking life* or *letting live* are the sovereign's fundamental attributes. But only when he actually kills —even tyrannically, unjustly—does the sovereign fully exert his symbolic rights over life. Foucault suggested that the punishment was all the more ruthless in that it was meant to offset the discontinuous hold of power over society. "The meshes of the net were too big," and eluded his grasp.[4] This *strategic* vision of domination went a long way in accounting for the technological mutation of power in the West at the dawn of the industrial revolution. While outwardly maintaining the image of sovereignty, a new type of disciplinary control sank deeper into the social body, down to its most tenuous elements. What disappeared in the process was symbolic exchange. Foucault's inversion of the system of power from the top down, from the sovereignty of death to the discipline of life, follows the same logic. The new system of power which replaced the old in the nineteenth century had its own claims: the right to *take* life and *let* die. Life replaced death as a means of controlling society at large.

Hegel's master/slave dialectics was based on the slave's fear of death. Giving it a perverse twist, Bataille hypothesized that there was not just one, but two separate forms of mastery. The first, relying on classical "domination," is geared to produce obedient subjects. The master rules because the slave is afraid of death, and he is not. But were the master to actually die, Bataille objected, he would lose his mastery. The master was no different

---

4. Michel Foucault, "Les mailles du pouvoir" (1976) in *Dits et écrits*, IV, Paris, Gallimard, 1994, p. 190.

from the slave, and dialectics was a con-game. Both were ruled by the fear. Bataille went on to hypothesize another form of sovereignty that would be *divorced from domination*. The real sovereign is *noble*, in the Nietzschean sense. He doesn't derive his power from his subjects, but from his own death. He only waits it to come, immune from any danger save the one who will murder him. It was in that way that Bataille managed to reestablish a symbolic exchange where there was none.

In 1933, Bataille extended this sacrificial economy to contemporary labor through his reading of Marcel Mauss's *The Gift*. Mauss opposed the "restricted economy" of capital (utility and use value) with the Northwestern American-Indian model of the "potlatch," a symbolic exchange in which goods are ritually destroyed and rivalry exacerbated to the point of terminal violence. For Bataille, only useless expenditure was able to counter the deadening effect of capital's exchangeability. The most lucid man, he wrote, will understand nothing if "it does not occur to him that a human society can have, just as he does, an *interest* in considerable losses, in catastrophes that, *while conforming to well-defined needs*, provoke tumultuous depressions, crises of dread, and, in the final analysis, a certain orgiastic state."[5]

---

5. Georges Bataille, in *Visions of Excess*, tr. Allan Stoekl, Minneapolis, University of Minnesota Press, 1985, p. 117.

Bataille looked upon capital as enslaving workers as being the same thing as the sovereign imposing obedience on his subjects. Just because the sovereign chose to *let* his subjects live didn't mean he let them free. They remained subjected to him in whatever function they carried out. Whether a prisoner of war, whose life was spared; a slave serving in sumptuary domesticity; an emancipated slave; or a serf in the fields, none of their lives were their own. They didn't have to die in order to be dead; their death was *differed*, kept in suspension, until the sovereign decided otherwise.

And the same holds true for the factory worker. Labor, Bataille maintained, was a unilateral gift of capital to the workers and was *meant* "to condemn them to a hideous degradation." Contrary to what Marx believed, the process of production wasn't set up to extract from them a surplus-value, its real purpose was to subject them to a sacrifice. And Bataille dismissed the American "subterfuge" of compensating workers for the debasement that had been imposed on them. Nothing could modify the fundamental division between noble and ignoble men. "The cruel game of social life does not vary among the different civilized countries, where the insulting splendor of the rich loses and degrades the human nature of the lower class."[6]

---

6. Georges Bataille, *Ibid*, p. 126.

And "the scenario has never changed," Baudrillard concurred, since labor power has been instituted on death. Having converted his death into a wage, the worker could only free himself by putting his own death on the line.

Whether the industrialists would crush their workers, or the workers slaughter their masters (it had been the dilemma in 1933 Germany) didn't matter that much to him as long as a sacrificial economy took over from political economy. "Whoever works *has not been put to death*, he is refused this honor," Baudrillard wrote in the same vein. The worst that capital could do to a worker is to keep him alive, condemned to "the indefinite abjection of a life of labor." [39]

Unlike Artaud and Bataille, his older contemporaries, Baudrillard never yearned for an inner experience of death reached through anguish, terror, or eroticism, yet he remained convinced that death *as a form internal to the system* was the only way left to offset it. As labor was slow death, only an instant and violent challenge could possibly free one from it. Against every "revolutionary" view, he insisted, "we must maintain that the only alternative to labor is not free time, or non-labor, it is sacrifice." [39]

In *Symbolic Exchange and Death*, Baudrillard remained indebted as well to Foucault's genealogy of exclusion, but he realized that every site of enclosure—asylums, prisons, factories, schools—would eventually be reabsorbed by the system and displayed as phantom references. Liberating madness, or sexuality, would simply empty them out of their subversive potential. In the late 1970s, Foucault and Guattari did their utmost to open the asylums, and succeeded all too well—mental patients were simply dumped into the streets. The same happened to sex, which became an industry. The only site left untouched was death. Or rather it was *disappeared* in broad daylight in order to leave room for the new consumer way of life. Instead of madness, the limit by which contemporary society defines itself became death. "Perhaps death and death alone," Baudrillard concluded, "belongs to a higher order than the code." [4] He didn't mean death as a biological fact, but the *reversibility* of death.

Etienne de la Boétie, a young Renaissance philosopher and close friend of Michel de Montaigne, wrote a slim pamphlet that has not ceased to fascinate generations of thinkers, Baudrillard included. The argument of La Boétie's *Discourse of Voluntary Servitude*, 1548, was simple, but powerful. How did it happen that "so many men, so many villages, so many cities, so many nations, sometimes suffer under a single tyrant who has no other power than the power they give him…"[7] What could have "denatured" men to such an extent that, born to live free, they would have lost "the remembrance of their original being, and the desire to regain it"? His answer was stark: people lose their freedom through their own blindness. The desire to serve the tyrant is something that they themselves want. Had La Boétie known about native societies discovered at the time in the New World (and maybe he did) it certainly would have vindicated his argument about the denaturation of humanity. It was proof enough that voluntary servitude wasn't innate, but prompted from the outside.

Something must have happened then, La Boétie suggested, a "misfortune" [*malencontre*] that made people willing, even eager, to embrace their tyrant. Suddenly domination caught on, affecting everyone, eventually wearing the face of the sovereign or the form of the State. As long as time was circular, and society undivided, the mechanism of servitude was kept in abeyance. The accident, or misfortune, knocked all this down. It was the beginning of History. "*All divided societies* are slave societies"[8] Pierre

7. Etienne de La Boétie, *Discourse on Voluntary Servitude*, trans. Harry Kurz, New York, Columbia University Press, 1942, p. 7.

8. Pierre Clastres, *The Archeology of Violence*, tr. Jeanine Herman, Los Angeles, Semiotext(e), 2010, p. 174.

Clastres, a controversial political anthropologist, concluded in *The Archeology of Violence*, "because this love of the subjects for the master equally denatures the relations between subjects."[9] The people's love for their own subjection became the well-hidden secret of domination. Every relation of power is oppressive, regardless of who, cruel or benevolent, comes to assume it.

In *Tristes Tropiques*, Claude Lévi-Strauss held on to the idea of "innocent savages" corrupted by Western civilization. It didn't prevent good natives from practicing tortures and scarifications with even more gusto and expertise than the sovereign's henchmen when they tore the regicide's flesh from his breast, or burnt it with wax and sulfur. But it wasn't for the benefit of one, distinct from the rest of the tribe. To the contrary: the ghastly ritual was meant to inscribe on native bodies the tribal law that everybody, without exception, would have to obey. The collective memory created through violence and death, wasn't buried deep inside them, but indelibly displayed on their skin for everyone to see. It certainly required extreme codifications on the part of Indian tribes to resist change and remain exempt from domination. Far from being close to nature, they subjected themselves to ferocious markings whose ultimate outcome, Clastres

---

9. *Ibid*, p. 187.

maintained, was to prevent the emergence in their midst of this cold monster, the State. Whether so-called primitive cultures had been exposed to savage empires beforehand, or preempted their recurrence through their own practices and institutions, remains an open debate, but they deliberately devised a number of strict mechanisms to that effect. To keep their numbers down, they engaged in ceaseless wars against neighboring tribes, and kept civil, religious and war powers separate. Primitive societies ignored slavery, and preserved as well their ancestral homeostasis by staging ritual destructions of accumulated wealth. This is what "potlatch" ultimately is about: eradicating the evil share, making sure that whoever wins the ruthless challenge would end up with nothing, and even less than nothing: losing their lives. Survivors acquired more prestige, but were too destitute to represent a serious threat.

The power attributed to chiefs in anthropological literature, from Marcel Mauss to Lévi-Strauss, has been wildly overestimated. In his celebrated "Writing Lesson,"[10] Lévi-Strauss recounts that he singled out the tribal chief by his superior intelligence and his eagerness to acquire power from the peculiar technology used by the anthropologist to

10. A chapter of Claude Lévi-Strauss, *Tristes Tropiques*, New York: Criterion Books, 1961, pp. 286–297.

consign his observations. There couldn't have been, of course, a greater betrayal in a society without writing and without history, where traditions were passed on orally from generation to generation, than to introduce writing, however rudimentary and ape-like. But someone, an insider, had to dissociate himself from his congeners and take on the blame for the stranger who came from the outside to break the secrets of the tribe. Lévi-Strauss automatically assumed that the chief, because a "chief," was different form the others, and willing to acquire from the foreigner a power that he would have been unable to devise on his own from within. Such was the price to pay for enlightenment, and Lévi-Strauss was eager to assume the White Man's guilt for it, as long as the savages retained their assumed naturalness. What sealed this little mental drama, and got the story straight, was the passing mention that the chief, ultimately, was decommissioned and expelled by his kin.

Contrary to the sovereign, Indian chiefs are remarkable for their complete lack of authority. The only power they own resides in the *palabra*, in their capacity to maintain by their speeches an equilibrium within the group. They recapitulate out loud, like a mantra, the tribe's genealogy and tradition, while no one, ostensibly, is paying attention. As Clastres says, he doesn't have the right, but the *duty* to talk. Chiefs have no power to *take* life, let alone appropriate some of the tribe's wealth. Actually, they have to divest themselves from everything they own, and tolerate a "permanent plunder" from the other members. No wonder the position of a chief is not exactly desirable. They remain dependent on everyone else, and are granted several women, not as a privilege, but because they aren't allowed to hunt for themselves. Generosity is not only a chief's duty, but "an involuntary servitude."

Deleuze and Guattari reproached Clastres (whom they consulted for *Anti-Oedipus*) for assuming that native societies could exist in autarchy outside of history. But Clastres did more: he suggested that La Boetie himself had pulled off a similar feat. The question that his *Discourse* raises, he said, is so "totally free" and independent of any territoriality that it can still be received today in the same way. La Boetie had a unique opportunity to "step out of history" because the monarchy was just beginning to emerge among rival feudal lords and divide society along a vertical axis, pitting against each other sovereigns and subjects, masters and slaves. In truth, specialists agree that the *Discourse* was a direct response to a massive peasant uprising against taxes in Guyenne, the first of its kind, that was ruthlessly crushed by the monarch's soldiers in 1548.

La Boetie's purpose wasn't to encourage subjects to rebel, but to remind them that any domination is illegitimate: "From all these indignities, such as the very beasts of the field would not endure, you can deliver yourselves if you try, not by taking action, but merely by willing to be free. Resolve to serve no more, and you are at once freed... support him no longer; then you will behold him, like a great Colossus whose pedestal has been pulled away, fall of his own weight and break in pieces." La Boetie showed no respect for the sovereign's right, divine or not, let alone for those who subjected themselves willingly to it. There was something that nothing could subdue, even under the most vicious tortures: the power that death affords. Montaigne, an exile like him in his own time, wrote: "Premeditation of death is premeditation of freedom... Acknowledging death frees us from every subjection and constraint." Only death resists domination.

Voluntary servitude is a paradoxical statement because servitude is not experienced passively, but actively—after all, it is willed. And anything that is willed could be unwilled. People rather desire their own oppression. Obviously, they must get something in return: identity, privilege, security, even pleasure, however perverse. Jean-François Lyotard once asserted, scandalously, in *Libidinal Economy*, that factory workers enjoyed their lot. They were *proles*, and proud to be. Didn't the proletariat, after Marx, become a value? They were the only ones who knew what "rough reality" was. French intellectuals, Jean-Paul Sartre included, felt deeply illegitimate, even dwarfed by them, and wore their blue overalls in demonstrations to appropriate some of their power. Philosopher Simone Weil couldn't care less about power, she just wanted to be crucified. She joined the assembly line to experience what being a slave was like and took herself for one, reinventing God in order to seal her own fate. Factory workers were the future of humankind—as if slavery could bring anything else than more slavery. In the end it wasn't the dictatorship of the proletariat that brought out a classless society, but capitalism—on its own terms, of course, and for its own benefit.

Voluntary servitude wasn't something that one could acknowledge, consciously or not; it was power turned inside out, everyone forever circling around each other. What was unforgivable about May '68 rebels or about the Autonomia movement at its peak in 1977 is that they did *not* want to take power. Franco Piperno, one of their leaders, admitted to me later on: "We didn't know what we would have done with it." As Baudrillard writes in *The Agony of Power*: "Power itself must be abolished—and not solely because of a refusal to be dominated, which is at the heart of all traditional struggles—but also, just as violently, in the refusal to dominate."

The Agony of Power

1

FROM DOMINATION TO HEGEMONY

In order to grasp how globalization and global antagonism works, we should distinguish carefully between domination and hegemony. One could say that hegemony is the ultimate stage of domination and its terminal phase. Domination is characterized by the master/slave relation, which is still a dual relation with potential alienation, a relationship of force and conflicts. It has a violent history of oppression and liberation. There are the dominators and the dominated—it remains a symbolic relationship. Everything changes with the emancipation of the slave and the internalization of the master by the emancipated slave. Hegemony begins here in the disappearance of the dual, personal, agonistic domination for the sake of integral reality—the reality of networks, of the virtual and total exchange where there are no longer dominators or dominated.

Indeed, it could be said that hegemony brings domination to an end. We, emancipated workers, internalize the Global Order and its operational setup of which we are the hostages far more than the slaves. Consensus, be it voluntary or involuntary, replaces traditional servitude, which still belongs to the symbolic register of domination.

"HEGEMON" means the one who commands, orders, leads and governs (and not the one who dominates and exploits). This brings us back to the literal meaning of the word "cybernetic" (*Kubernetikè*, the art of governing). Contrary to domination, a hegemony of world power is no longer a dual, personal or real form of domination, but the domination of networks, of calculation and integral exchange.

Domination can be overthrown from the outside. Hegemony can only be inverted or reversed from the inside. Two different, almost contrary paradigms: the paradigm of revolution, transgression, subversion (domination) and the paradigm of inversion, reversion, auto-liquidation (hegemony). They are almost exclusive of each other, because the mechanisms of revolution, of anti-domination, as history demonstrated, can become the impetus or the vector for hegemony. We could compare hegemony to the brain, which is its biological equivalent. Like the brain, which subordinates every other function, the central computer assumes the hegemonic hold of a global power and can therefore serve as an image of our present political situation.

What other feature distinguishes hegemony from pure and simple domination is the coming of a fundamental event: simulacra and simulation. Hegemony works through general masquerade, it relies on the excessive use of every sign and obscenity, the way it mocks its own values, and challenges the rest of the world by its cynicism ("carnivalization"). Classical, historical domination imposed a system of positive values, displaying as well as defending these values. Contemporary hegemony, on the other hand, relies on a symbolic liquidation of every possible value. The terms "simulacrum," "simulation" and "virtual" summarize this liquidation, in which every signification is eliminated in its own sign, and the profusion of signs parodies a by now unobtainable reality. This is the total masquerade in which domination itself is engulfed. Power is only the parody of the signs of power—just as war is only the parody of signs of war, including technology. Masquerade of war, masquerade of power. We can therefore speak of the hegemony of masquerade, and the masquerade of hegemony. All meaning is abolished in its own sign and the profusion of signs parodies a now undiscoverable reality.

Domination and hegemony are separated by the liquidation of reality, the super fast irruption, of late, of a global principle of simulation, a global hold by the virtual. Globalization is the hegemony of a global power and can only occur in the framework of the virtual and the networks—with the homogeneity that comes from signs emptied of their substance.

The entire Western masquerade relies on the cannibalization of reality by signs, or of a culture by itself. I use "cannibalize" here in the derivative sense of *cannibalizing a car*, using it as spare parts. Cannibalizing a culture, as we do it today, means tinkering with its values like spare parts inasmuch as the entire system is out of order. This distinction between domination and hegemony is crucial. It determines the forms of resistance appropriate for each and the various ways in which the present situation could evolve. One doesn't respond to hegemony and domination in the same way; the strategies should not be confused.

In the face of this hegemony, the work of the negative, the work of critical thought, of the relationship of forces against oppression, or of radical subjectivity against alienation, all this has (virtually) become obsolete. It has become obvious that, thanks to the twists and turns of cynical reason, or the ruses of history, this new hegemonic configuration (which is no longer the hegemony of capital) has absorbed the negative, negativity as a way of regaining the initiative. Caught in a vast Stockholm syndrome, the alienated, the oppressed, and the colonized are siding with the system that holds them hostage. They are now "annexed," in the literal sense, prisoners of the "nexus," of the network, connected for better or worse.

Power has ransacked all of the strategies of simulation: parody, irony, and self-mockery—leaving the Left with only a phantom of the truth. The famous slogan for the Banque Nationale de Paris (BNP) in the 1970s comes to mind: "Your money interests me!" This statement encapsulates the ignominy of capital far better than any critical analysis. Denouncing capital and all of the banking mechanisms was nothing new, the scandalous feature was that the banker himself had said it; truth coming out from the mouth of Evil. It wasn't a denunciation, a critical analysis. It came from the dominant power and enjoyed complete immunity. It could admit its "crime" in broad daylight.

The most recent profession of faith in a similar vein came from Patrick Le Lay, CEO of TF1, the French television channel: "Let's be realistic: the job of TF1 is to help Coca-Cola sell its products. For an advertising campaign to work properly, the viewer's brains have to be accessible. The goal of our programs is to make them available, by entertaining them, relaxing them between two messages. What we sell to Coca-Cola is relaxed-brains time... Nothing is harder than getting them to open up."

We should pay our respect to this amazing admission and professional cynicism. It is widely shared, as the following slogan for Poste Télécom testifies: "Money has no sex, but it will reproduce." And it could be condemned for the same reason, as it was by all fine minds. But this is not the real problem. Even those who condemned Le Lay's shocking statement were fascinated by its insolence. Doesn't this shameless flippancy mani-fest a greater freedom than the stonewalling of critical contestation? But this is the question: how could truth be lifted by an "arrogant" dis-course that gets the upper-hand by short-circuiting any critique?

Technocratic cynicism is not scandalous *per se*, but by the way it breaks a fundamental rule of our social and political game: corruption for some and protesting Evil for others. If the corrupt have no respect for this protocol, and show their hand without sparing us their hypocrisy, then the ritual mechanism of denunciation goes haywire. The privilege of telling the truth eludes our grasp—in the face of capital unveiled by the capitalists, even.

In fact, Le Lay takes away the only power we had left. He steals our denunciation. *This* is the real scandal. Otherwise, how could you explain the general outrage when he revealed an open secret?

Instead of denouncing evil from the position of the good (eternal moral position), he expresses evil from the position of evil. It is the best way to say it, but it remains inadmissible. Truth must be on the side of Good. There can be no intelligence on the side of Evil. Yet all those who outdo themselves with arrogance (Le Pen), cynicism (Le Lay), pornography (Abu Ghraib), mythomania (Marie L.) unmask the truth of the system in their abuse of it. The effects are both fascinating and revolting—and they are much more effective than conventional critiques.

A bitter truth: radicalness is on the side of the intelligence of evil. Critical intelligence no longer measures up to the collapse of reality and to the passage into total reality. The truth, or the inhumanity of this situation, can only be revealed from the inside, voluntarily or involuntarily, by the agents of the embezzlement of reality. Only evil can speak evil now—evil is a ventriloquist. Critical intelligence is left to jump over its own shadow: even in its radicalness, it remains pious and denunciatory. The curse of critical discourse is to reconcile itself secretly with those it criticizes by denouncing them (and I am well aware that what I am saying here belongs to this discourse). Denunciation will never have the shocking frankness of an unscrupulous discourse. We must look to the side of evil for the clearest indications, the harshest reality. Only those who show no concern for contradiction or critical consideration in their acts and discourse can, by this very means, shed full light, without remorse or ambiguity, on the absurd and extravagant character of the state of things, through the play of objective irony.

What is happening to critical thought—the thought of the Enlightenment and the Revolution, the thought that drove the analysis of capital, merchandise and spectacle throughout the nineteenth and twentieth centuries—is what happened before to religious, ethnic and linguistic phenomena. We are presently witnessing their formal renewal, but without any of their original substance. The religious revival is epigonal and has nothing to do with the fervor of past centuries. It presupposes the dilution of faith as symbolic organization, the disappearance of transcendence (and maybe even the death of God). It is the specific product of a disenchanted situation of loss where everything that disappears is artificially revived. It is the abreactive product of a world where there is no reason left to believe in anything.

Current critical thought continues along its trajectory but it is no longer the critical thought of the Enlightenment and modernity, which had their own object and their own energy. It is merely an epiphenomenon of a world where there is nothing left to analyze in the hopes of subverting it. This thought is no longer current because we are no longer in a "critical" situation, like the historical domination of capital. We have entered a hegemonic form of total reality, of closed-circuit global power that has even captured the negative. All that is left today is the specific product of this posthumous situation where it no longer has a historical reason to exist or any effectiveness.

Yet it is all the more prominent. The critique of alienation and spectacle has blossomed and spread to the point that it has become the most common vulgate because it is the only discourse of consolation that we have. But its tone has changed; it has become more melancholy as subversion and transgression have lost popularity today.

Three simultaneous dimensions form the passage from domination to hegemony. It is a perilous triple jump, a three-part sacrifice:

1) Capital surpasses itself and turns against itself in the sacrifice of value (the economic illusion).
2) Power turns against itself in the sacrifice of representation (the democratic illusion).
3) The entire system turns against itself in the sacrifice of reality (the metaphysical illusion).

All three jump over their shadow.

The shadow of capital is value. The shadow of power is representation. The shadow of the system is reality. They respectively move beyond Value, Representation and Reality—in a hyperspace that is no longer economic, political or real but rather the hegemonic sphere.

Capital is both the total realization of Value and its liquidation. Power is now the final form of representation: it only represents itself. The system is the total version of the Real and at the same time its liquidation through the Virtual. This is the hegemonic form.

The Economic Illusion

In any event, the question of "capital" must be reconfigured. Does something like capital still exist, and, if there is a crisis, what is the essence of this crisis? We must try to pass "through the looking glass," beyond the mirror of production.

Does exploitation still exist? Can we still talk about alienation? Have we become the hostages (not the slaves, but the hostages) of a global market under the definitive sign of globalization? But can we still talk of a "market"? And hasn't capitalism reached the point of destroying the conditions of its own existence?

One of the problems of generalized exchange is that the market is both its ideal and its strategic location. It may be the fatal destiny of capital to go to the limit of exchange—to the total consumption of reality. In its historical (and Marxist) definition, capitalism presided over the multiplication of exchanges in the name of value. The market obeys the law of value and equivalency. The limit here is the limit of classic capitalism. And the crises of capital can always be resolved by regulating value.

This is no longer true for the financial flows and international speculation that far surpass the laws of the market. Can we still speak of capital? Do we keep the term and the concept and therefore acknowledge the exponential strategy that pushes capital beyond its own limits, into a whirlwind of exchanges where capital loses its very essence which is the essence of the market—and self-destructs in an unbridled circulation that brings the very concept of exchange to an end? Or do we consider that it is no longer capital at all but something radically different, an exchange that is not only general but total—completely freed from value and markets—an exchange that, having lost its rational principle, the principle of value, becomes integral just as reality, having lost its reality principle, becomes integral reality, from which there is no salvation?

In this light, capital in its historical form appears to be a lesser evil. In relation to a virtual universe, reality appears to be a lesser evil. In view of hegemony, domination itself appears to be a lesser evil. Take the example of the Web, the Internet, networks, blogs, etc. It is all free, "liberally" deployed without economic constraints, beyond markets, in a frenzy of total communication. This is a virtual catastrophe, the catastrophe of total exchange that is not even protected by money or the market. We find ourselves wanting it all to be subject to the law of value, taken in hand by capitalist power, to slow its exponential development, to escape the ecstasy of (free, secular and obligatory) communication—because it is leading to the dictatorship of forced exchange—but no one will escape.

The next stage, which can be seen in these mysteriously free networks, is much worse than anything that was stigmatized as the mercantilization of exchange, where everything is assigned a price and a market. This influence (which is not strictly speaking the influence of a person, a "capitalist" power or any political power) is the ascendancy of total, integral free exchange, universal wiring, universal connection. Capital, markets, surplus value, merchandise and prices seem like a lesser evil or protection against something worse. This is the virtual dimension of hegemony—

it is different from the domination of capital and different from the dimension of power in its strictly political definition.

The Democratic Illusion

One might wonder, however, if hegemony is a direct continuation or perpetuation of domination. Is it the same form deployed to its ultimate consequences? Or is there a moment where there is a shift to a noncritical form—beyond internal crises but not exempt from internal catastrophe or self-dissolution through saturation (like any system at the limit of its possibilities). A world of total, instantaneous, perpetual communication is unthinkable and, in any case, intolerable.

Hegemony corresponds to a phase of the saturation of power (political, financial, military and even cultural power) pushed by its own logic but unable to accomplish its possibilities fully—a dire fate indeed (the story of the umbrella—maybe the dire fate of realizing possibilities fully is the fate of humankind?). Yet any action that tries to slow capital or power, that tries to keep them from accomplishing all of their possibilities is their last hope, their last chance to survive "just short of their end." And if we let them, they will rush headlong to their end (taking us with them).

Is it better to let them do it, to let them follow their fatal penchant for self-destruction through saturation and ultra-realization—or is it better to slow them down to avoid disaster? This is the paradox we confront in the paroxysm of power. (And, once again, the same global, universal problem faces humanity and its "hypertelic" fate when it rushes to its end because it is too successful [technologically, sexually, demographically, etc.])

It all depends on your idea of power. If you presuppose that intelligence or the imagination hold power, then the persistence of stupidity or at least the permanent absence of imagination from power is inexplicable. (Unless you also suppose a general disposition among people to delegate their sovereignty to the most inoffensive, least imaginative of their fellow citizens, a *malin génie* that pushes people to elect the most nearsighted, corrupt person out of a secret delight in seeing the stupidity and corruption of those in power. Especially in times of trouble, people will vote massively for the candidate who does not ask them to think. It is a silent conjuration, analogous in the political sphere to the conspiracy of art in another domain.)

We should abandon the democratic illusion of imagination or intelligence in power that comes from the depths of Enlightenment ideology. The naïve utopias of the 1960s must be revised:

"Imagination in power!"—"Take your dreams for reality!"—"No limits to pleasure!" All of these slogans were realized (or hyperrealized) in the development of the system.

If we remove the moral utopia of power—power as it should be in the eyes of those who reject it—if we hypothesize that power only lives through parody or simulations of representation and is defined by the society that manipulates it; if we accept the hypothesis that power is an ectoplasmic, yet indispensable function, then people like Bush or Schwarzenegger fill their roles perfectly. Not that a country or a people has the leaders it deserves but that the leaders are an emanation of global power. The political structure of the United States is in direct correlation to its global domination. Bush leads the United States in the same way as those who exercise global hegemony over the rest of the planet. (We could even say that the hegemony of global power resembles the absolute privilege of the human species over all others.) There is therefore no reason to think of an alternative.

Power itself must be abolished—and not solely in the refusal to be dominated, which is at the heart of all traditional struggles—but also, just as violently, in the refusal to dominate (if the refusal to dominate had the same violence and the same energy as the refusal to be dominated, the dream of revolution would have disappeared long ago). Intelligence cannot, can never be in power because intelligence consists of this double refusal. "If I could think that there were a few people without any power in the world, then I would know that all is not lost" (Elias Canetti).

The Metaphysical Illusion

The reabsorption of critical negativity is echoed by an even more radical form of denial: the denial of reality.

In simulation, you move beyond true and false through parody, masquerade, derision to form an immense enterprise of deterrence. Deterrence from every historical reference, from all reality in the passage into signs. This strategy of destabilization, of discrediting, of divestment from reality in the form of parody, mockery, or masquerade becomes the very principle of government, is also a depreciation of all value.

The question is no longer of a power or a "political" power connected to a history, to forms of representation, to contradictions and a critical alternative. Representation has lost its principle and the democratic illusion is complete—not as much by the violation of rights as by the simulation of values, general uncertainty and the derealization of all reality. Everyone is caught in the signs of power that occupy the entire space—and that are shared by everyone communally (take for example the resigned, embarrassed complicity in the rigged workings of the political sphere and polls).

From there, the system works exponentially:

—not starting from value, but from the liquidation of value.
—not through representation, but through the liquidation of representation.
—not from reality but from the liquidation of reality.

Everything in the name of which domination was exercised is terminated, sacrificed, which should logically lead to the end of domination. This is indeed the case, but for the sake of hegemony.

The system doesn't care a fig for laws; it unleashes deregulation in every domain.

—Deregulation of value in speculation.
—Deregulation of representation in the various forms of manipulation and parallel networks.
—Deregulation of reality through information, the media and virtual reality.

From that point on: total immunity—one can no longer counter the system in the name of one's own principles since the system has abolished them. The end of all critical negativity. Closure of every account and all history. The reign of hegemony. On the contrary, since it is no longer regulated by representation, or its own concept, or the image of itself, the system succumbs to the final temptation: it becomes hypersensitive to its final conditions and casts itself beyond its own end according to the inflexible decrease of the rates of reality.

The most serious of all forms of self-denial—not only economically or politically but metaphysically—is the denial of reality. This immense enterprise of deterrence from every historical reference, this strategy of discrediting, of divesting from reality in the form of parody, mockery, or masquerade, becomes the very principle of government. The new strategy—and it truly is a mutation—is the self-immolation of value, of every system of value, of self-denial, indifferentiation, rejection and nullity as the triumphant command.

Moreover, the concept of the universal is the specific product, within the human race, of a certain civilization called Western, and within that culture, of a privileged minority, a modern intelligentsia that has dedicated itself to the philosophical and technical edification of humanity. But what can this concept mean, not only outside the human race (it is irrelevant for the animal, plant or cosmic realms, the inhuman in general) but also in the major cultures other than our own (archaic, traditional or Eastern or Far-Eastern that do not even have a term for it) or even in our own societies outside the civilized and cultivated classes where humanism and universal principles have become hereditary. What does the universal mean in the eyes of immigrants, populations left fallow, entire zones of fracture and exclusion in our own "overdeveloped" societies? And even in the privileged fringe, the high-tech globality, what does the universal mean for all the "corporate people," all the high performance groups or individuals according to both a global and an increasingly corporate, isolationist, protectionist evolution?

Contrary to what Immanuel Kant said, the starry sky laughs at this universal law, but so does the heart of humankind: not only living beings but the vast majority of humans never obeyed it. And those who claim to obey it happily put their singular passions before any other ideal finality—this is no doubt, despite the concept, a more authentic way to be "human." Do they themselves believe in this ideal finality? No one knows; the only sure thing is that they claim to make others obey.

The discourse of the universal describes a tautological spiral: it is held by the species that considers itself superior to all others and within this species, by a minority that considers itself the holder of moral and universal ends, forming a veritable, "democratic" feudality.

Whatever the case may be, there is a major inconsistency in continuing to use a discourse of the universal as a discourse of reference when it has no meaning or effect anywhere—neither with global power nor in opposition to it.

To relativize our concept of the universal: with the increasing globalization of the world, discrimination becomes more ferocious.

The cartography should not confuse these zones beyond reality with those that still give signs of reality in the same hegemonic system of globalization, even though they do not function in the same way. We could even say that the gap separating them is growing and something that was only a cultural singularity in a non-unified world becomes real discrimination in a globalized universe. The more the world is globalized, the worst the discrimination.

The two universes, the hyperreal and the infrareal, seem to interpenetrate but are light years away from each other. The deepest misery and enclaves of luxury coexist in the same geographic space (take, for example the oil condominiums in Saudi Arabia and the favelas of Rio, but these are extreme cases). In fact, the entire planet is organized on the principle of definitive discrimination between two universes—which no longer have any knowledge of each other. Global power keeps its integral control over the other world, and has all the means necessary for its extermination. It is the tear in the universal. As for the consequences of this tear, the upheaval it can create, we have no idea—except for what is already present today (although it is only the beginning): the only response to this increasingly violent discrimination is an equally violent form, terrorism. An extreme reaction to this situation of impossible exchange.

Which leads us to Europe. In its current form, Europe is a nonevent. It was first an idea (maybe starting in the Middle Ages, a reality before an idea?). Now it is no longer an idea or a reality but a virtual reality referring to a model of simulation to which it must adapt. From the perspective of projection at any price, the will of the people is an obstacle or at least an indifferent parameter or an alibi. The "yes" vote comes from on high, and we can now see that the people are Europe's skeleton in the closet.

This virtual Europe is a caricature of global power. It wants to find its niche in the world order, to represent an economic power that rivals the ridiculous image of its American Big Brother. Europe is organized according to the same liberal principles, and other than a few last gasps of sentimental socialism, is aligned with the model of flux and global deregulation. It is incapable of inventing a new rule for the game (which is also the struggle of the Left on the national level).

Without its own political structure or historical reason, Europe can only desire expansion and proliferation into the void through indefinite "democratic" annexation, just like global power. Of course, all of the peripheral countries want to join this by-product of globalization, just as Europeans dream of reaching the global level.

Europeans have the same relationship to American global power as other countries (like Turkey, for example) have to Europe. Turkey's entry into Europe, outside any political considerations, may be revealing in terms of this paradox: Europeans "from birth" are not really modern either; they have not truly entered hyper-modernity. They are in fact resisting it, and in every country there is something that resists generalized exchange, the vertigo of universal exchange.

Is it good or bad? Does Europe have to be

resolutely modern? Should it resist the grasp of hegemony, while being its best accomplices?

Turkey wanting to enter Europe is not the least of the paradoxes at a time when France is giving signs of wanting to leave. The sudden rise of the "No" vote during the referendum was significant in this regard. It is the best example of a vital or visceral reaction in defense against the consensual blackmail of the "Yes," against the referendum's ultimatum in disguise. There is no need to have a political conscience to have this reflex: it is the automatic rekindling of negativity in the face of excessive positivity, to the coalition of "divine" Europe, the Europe of good conscience, the one on the right side of universality—with all others cast into the shadows of history.

The forces of Good were completely wrong about the perverse effects of an excess of Good and the unconscious lucidity that tells us to "never side with those who are already right." A good example of a response to hegemony that is not the work of the negative or the result of critical thought (the political reasons of the "No" are no better than those of the "Yes"). It is a response in the form of a pure and simple challenge to the saturation of the system, the implementation (once again, beyond political considerations) of a principle of reversion, of reversibility against the hegemonic principle. A good example of the "parallax of Evil."

We have here the profile of the new type of confrontation characterizing the era of Hegemony. It is not a class struggle or a fight for liberation on the global level (since the "liberation" of exchange and democracy, which were the counterpoint to domination, are the strategies of hegemony. Take, for example, England's presence in Zanzibar: by freeing the slaves in the late nineteenth century, England was able to take control of East Africa). It is an irreducibility, an irreducible antagonism to the global principle of generalized exchange.

In other words, a confrontation that is no longer precisely political but metaphysical and symbolic in the strong sense. It is a confrontation, a divide that exists not only at the heart of the dominant power, but at the heart of our individual existence.

—April 2005

2

THE WHITE TERROR OF WORLD ORDER

Absorbing the negative continues to be the problem. When the emancipated slave internalizes the master, the work of the negative is abolished. Domination becomes hegemony. Power can show itself positively and overtly in good conscience and complete self-evidence. It is unquestionable and global. But the game is not over yet. For while the slave internalizes the master, power also internalizes the slave who denies it, and it denies itself in the process. Negativity reemerges as irony, mocking and auto-liquidation internal to power. This is how the slave devours and cannibalizes the Master from the inside. As power absorbs the negative, it is devoured by what it absorbs. There is justice in reversibility.

A catastrophic dialectic has replaced the "work of the negative." Critical thought, or any attempt to attack the system from the inside, is in a complete aporia. After voluntary servitude, which was the secret key to exercising domination, one could now speak instead of involuntary complicity, consensus and connivance with the World Order by everything that seems to oppose it. Images, even radical-critical ones, are still a part of the crime they denounce, albeit an involuntary one. What is the impact of a film like *Darwin's Nightmare*, which denounces racial discrimination in Tanzania? It will tour the Western world and reinforce the endogamy, the cultural and political autarky of this separate world through images and the consumption of images.

And yet by the same token all critical negativity, all the work of the negative is abolished, devoured by signs and simulacra. In the context of hegemony, the historical work of critical thought, the relationship of forces against oppression, radical subjectivity against alienation are all (virtually) in the past. Simply because this new hegemonic configuration (which is no longer the configuration of capitalism at all) has itself absorbed the negative and used it for a leap forward through the meanders of cynical reasoning or the tricks of history.

The absolute negative (terrorism, internal deterrence) responds to the absolute positive of positivized power. When domination becomes hegemony, negativity becomes terrorism. Thus hegemony is a meta-stable form because it has absorbed the negative—but by the same token, lacking the possibility of dialectical balance, it remains infinitely fragile. Its victory, therefore, is only apparent, and its total positivity, this resorption of the negative, anticipates its own dissolution. It is therefore both the twilight of critical thought and the agony of power.

Through a reverse effect, however, the system enters a catastrophic dialectic. But this dialectic is a far cry from the Marxist dialectic and the teleological role of negation.

For this strategy of development and growth is fatal. As it entirely fulfills itself, in a final achievement that no negativity can hinder, it becomes incapable of surpassing itself "upwards" (*Aufhebung*) and initiates a process of self-annihilation (*Aufhebung* in the sense of dissolution).

For the system (in the context of global power), this strategy of development and growth is fatal. The system cannot prevent its destiny from being accomplished, integrally realized, and therefore driven into automatic self-destruction by the ostensible mechanisms of its reproduction.

Its shape is similar to what is called "turbo-capitalism." The term "turbo" should be taken literally in this expression. It means that the system as a whole is no longer driven by historical forces but is absorbed by its final conditions—

hastened to its definitive end (like a turbo engine sucking in the space in front of it, creating a vacuum and the force of attraction of a vacuum). It is not a progressive, continuous evolution, even if it is confrontational and contradictory. Instead, it is a vertiginous, irresistible attraction to its own end.

If negativity is totally engulfed by the system, if there is no more work of the negative, positivity sabotages itself in its completion. At the height of its hegemony, power cannibalizes itself—and the work of the negative is replaced by an immense work of mourning.

We can even forget about capital and capitalism. Didn't they reach the point where they would destroy their own conditions of existence? Can we still speak of a "market" or even of a classical economy? In its historical definition, capitalism presided over the multiplication of exchanges under the auspices of value. The market obeys the law of value and equivalency. And the crises of capital can always be resolved by regulating value.

This is no longer true for the financial flows and international speculation that far surpass the laws of the market. Can we still speak of capital when faced with an exponential strategy that pushes capital beyond its limits in a whirlwind of exchanges where it loses its very essence and is dispersed in an unbridled circulation that brings the very concept of exchange to an end?

Having lost its rational principle, the principle of value, exchange becomes total just as reality, having lost its reality principle, becomes total reality. It may be the fatal destination of capital to go to the end of exchange—toward a total consumption of reality. In any case, we are bound for this generalized exchange, this frenetic communication and information that is the sign of hegemony.

The dimension of hegemony is different from that of capital and different from the dimension of power in its strictly political definition. It is no longer a question of political power tied to a history and a form of representation. Representation itself has lost its principle and the democratic illusion is complete. Not through the violation of rights but through the simulation of values and the derealization of all reality. The masquerade again, everyone caught in the signs of power and communing in the rigged unfolding of the political stage.

With the election of Arnold Schwarzenegger as Governor of California, we are deep in the masquerade, where politics is only a game of idolatry and marketing. It is a giant step toward the end of the system of representation. This is the destiny of contemporary politicians—those who live by the show will die by the show. This is true for both "citizens" and politicians. It is the immanent justice of the media. You want the power of the image? Then you will die through its replay. The carnival of the image is also (self) cannibalization through the image.

One should not conclude too hastily that the degradation of American political practices is a decline in power. Behind this masquerade, there is a vast political strategy (certainly not deliberate; it would require too much intelligence) that belies our eternal democratic illusions. By electing Schwarzenegger (or in Bush's rigged election in 2000), in this bewildering parody of all systems of representation, America took revenge for the disdain of which it is the object. In this way, it proved its imaginary power because no one can equal it in its headlong course into the democratic masquerade, into the nihilist enterprise of liquidating value and a more total simulation than even in the areas of finance and weapons. America has a long head start. This extreme, empirical and technical form of mockery and the profanation of values, this radical obscenity and total impiety of a people, otherwise known as "religious," this is what fascinates everyone. This is what we enjoy even through rejection and sarcasm: this phenomenal vulgarity, a (political, televisual) universe brought to the zero degree of culture. It is also the secret of global hegemony.

I say it without irony, even with admiration: this is how America, through radical simulation, dominates the rest of the world. It serves as a model while taking its revenge on the rest of the world, which is infinitely superior to it in symbolic terms. The challenge of America is the challenge of desperate simulation, of a masquerade it imposes on the rest of the world, including the desperate *simulacrum* of military power. Carnivalization of power. And that challenge cannot be met: we have neither a finality or a counter-finality that can oppose it.

In its hegemonic function, power is a virtual configuration that metabolizes any element to serve its own purposes. It could be made of countless intelligent particles, but its opaque structure would not change. It is like a body that changes its cells constantly while remaining the same. Soon, every molecule of the American nation will have come from somewhere else, as if by transfusion. America will be Black, Indian, Hispanic, and Puerto Rican while remaining America. It will be all the more mythically American in that it will no longer be "authentically" American. And all the more fundamentalist in that it will no longer have a foundation (even though it never had one, since even the Founding Fathers came from somewhere else). And all the more bigoted in that it will have become, in fact, multiracial and multicultural. And all the more imperialist in that it will be led by the descendants of slaves. That is the subtle and unassailable logic of power; it cannot be changed.

This global masquerade of power passes through several phases. First, in the name of universals, the West imposes its political and economic models on the entire world along with its principle of technical rationality. That was the essence of its domination but not yet its quintessence. Beyond economics and politics, its quintessence relies on the hold of simulation, an operational simulation of every value, every culture—that is where hegemony today asserts itself. No longer through exporting techniques, values, ideologies but through the universal extrapolation of a parody of these values. Underdeveloped countries keep aligning themselves on a simulacrum of development and growth; they get their independence from a simulacrum of democracy, and every endangered culture dreams of a staged rehabilitation—all fascinated by the same universal model (of which America, while benefiting from it, is the first victim). Thus, after imposing its domination through History, the West is now imposing its hegemony through the FARCE of History. Global power is the power of the simulacrum.

Moreover, Western civilization also had a motive for revenge. It had to take revenge on others for the loss of its own values (many people underestimate the fierce jealousy mixed with nostalgia of a disenchanted culture for all singular cultures). And it continues to do so in the context of globalization which, at bottom, beyond its technical operation, is a giant project meant to symbolically liquidate all values through consensus or force.

After the sacrifice of value, after the sacrifice of representation, after the sacrifice of reality, the West is now characterized by the deliberate sacrifice of everything through which a human being keeps some value in his or her own eyes.

The terrorists' potlatch against the West is their own death. Our potlatch is indignity, immodesty, obscenity, degradation and abjection. This is the movement of our culture—where the stakes keep rising. Our truth is always on the side of unveiling, desublimation, reductive analysis—the truth of the repressed—exhibition, avowal, nudity—nothing is true unless it is desecrated, objectified, stripped of its aura, or dragged onstage.

Indifferentiation of values but also indifference to ourselves. We cannot involve our own death because we already are dead. We throw this indifference and abjection at others like a challenge: the challenge to defile themselves in return, to deny their values, to strip naked, confess, admit—

to respond with a nihilism equal to our own. We try to take it all from them by force: through the humiliations of Abu Ghraib, prohibiting veils in school. But it is not enough for our victory: they have to come on their own, sacrifice themselves on the altar of obscenity, transparency, pornography and global simulation; they have to lose their symbolic defenses and take the path of neoliberal order, total democracy and integrated spectacle.

In this sense, we can, with Boris Groys, conceive of the hypothesis of a double potlatch: the Western potlatch of nullity, self-degradation, shame, and mortification opposed to the terrorist potlatch of death. But the deliberate sacrifice by the West of all its values, of everything through which a culture holds value in its own eyes, in this prostitution of the self thrown into the face of the Other as a weapon of mass deterrence—seduction through emptiness and challenge to the Other (Islam, but also the rest of the world) to prostitute itself in return, to unveil itself, to give up all its secrets and lose all sovereignty—does this immense self-immolation constitute a veritable symbolic response to the challenge of the terrorists? (Let's not speak of war or a fight "against evil," which are admissions of a total inability to respond symbolically to the challenge of death.)

Potlatch versus potlatch—does one balance the other? One might say that one is a potlatch by excess (the potlatch of death) and the other a potlatch by default (self-mockery and shame). In that case, they do not match each other equally and one should speak of an asymmetrical potlatch. Or should one think that, in the end, no form, not even the challenge of death, of extreme sacrifice, can be considered superior, nor can the terrorist challenge be seen as superior to the inverse Western challenge, and therefore send each one back to its respective delirium?

What is at stake in global confrontation is this provocation to generalized exchange, the unbridled exchange of all differences, the challenge for other cultures to equal us in deculturation, the debasement of values, the adhesion to the most disenchanted models. This confrontation is not quite a "clash of civilizations," but it is not economic or political either, and today it only concerns the West and Islam in appearance. Fundamentally, it is a duel, and its stakes are symbolic: physical and mental liquidation, a universal carnivalization imposed by the West at the cost of its own humiliation, its symbolic expropriation—against all of the singularities that resist it. Challenge versus challenge? Potlatch versus potlatch? Does the slow-death strategy or systematic mortification equal the stakes of a sacrificial death? Can this confrontation come to an end and what could be the consequences if one or the other wins?

The response to domination is well known: slave revolt, class struggle, all the historical forms of revolt and revolution—the metamorphoses of the work of the negative. History, as we knew it and rewrote it along its evolution to an ideal end. The response to hegemony is not as simple: irredentism, dissidence, antagonism, violent abreaction—but also fascination and total ambivalence. For we all are part and parcel of this hegemony (unlike the clear distinction between dominants and dominated).

Whence both a vital, visceral resistance to generalized exchange, to total equivalence and connection, to vast prostitution and a vertiginous attraction to this technological fair, this spectacular masquerade, this nullity. At bottom it is clear that this apogee of global power is also the apotheosis of the negative, the triumph of resignation, of the renunciation by the species of its own values. There is nothing more exciting than this vertigo—no longer the work of the negative but the vertigo of denial and artifice! Whence this dual, insoluble postulate: opposing this global power and losing oneself in it. An ambivalence that we all experience at each moment and which is the mirror in each one of us of the global antagonism.

This hegemonic simulation, a configuration that seems triumphant and unyielding, has its reverse, its revulsive effects. By virtually yielding to this global dynamic and exaggerating it in several ways, all of these would-be emerging countries gradually become submerging instead. They slowly invade the Western sphere, not on a competitive level, but like a ground swell.

This invasion occurs in many ways, like a viral infiltration. It is the problem of global, more or less clandestine immigration (Hispanics are literally cannibalizing the United States). But also in the contemporary forms of terror, a true filterable virus, made up of terrorism and counterterrorism, and which is a violent abreaction to global domination, destabilizing it from the inside. The global order is cannibalized by terror.

However, there are other, more political forms for these tendencies hostile to Western models. All of these countries that we want to acculturate by force with the principles of political and economic rationality, with the global market and democracy, with a universal principle and a history that is not their own, of which they have neither the ends nor the means—all of these countries which make up the rest of the world—they give us the impression (in Brazil for example) that they will never be accultured to this exogenous model of calculation and growth, that they are deeply allergic to it. And in fact do we, Westerners, masters of the world, still have its ends and means? Do we still measure up to this universal undertaking of mastery that now seems to surpass us in every domain and function like a trap of which we are the first victims?

History itself is a product for Western export. We dump on others a desire for history (through national conflicts, international institutions, access to the global market) while for us, in reality, history is over, in the sense that it unfolds on its own, on automatic pilot and more often than not in a loop. For us, the mirror of history, the continuity of history is shattered; we live in an instant and disincarnate currentness in which we take no more trouble, according to Dostoyevsky's phrase, than to prolong history or rather the end of history, immersed in the euphoric banality that Heidegger called the second Fall of humanity. But the others, those who did not experience this historic stage, this mirror stage, can only want to enjoy it themselves—dreaming of the Western power in which everything that took the form of history culminates, and perhaps dreaming to destroy its symbols and take a stand against it. It is a strange situation wherein all these peoples who at the same time dream of entering history, or rather today in the pacified, securized, extraterritorial, extranational zone of universal free trade, in the World Order of Welfare of which America is obviously the model, and simultaneously resist it. A double contradictory statement of which Turkey is a fine example: to join Europe for the Turks means leaving an archaic structure to enter modernity, to become a part of the technological universe of consumerism and simulation, of the cosmopolitan exchange of signs and the formal liberty to use them at one's leisure. At the same time, it means partaking in a radical critique of this political economy, a denunciation of the culture that fascinates them and remaining deeply allergic to the principle of exchange and undifferentiated exchange that requires the sacrifice of their distinctive cultural traits.

In the end, if we look closely, it's the same situation we are in as individuals at the heart of modern societies—we all experience an irresistible urge for this society of signs and simulacra that is at the end of history and a deep resistance to this voluntary servitude. So much so that we might retrospectively wonder whether all this history, all of this Western rationality and modernity really took place or whether this is all a parody of an event that had happened, leaving us to share its spoils. This would be the "farce" of history that Marx mentions and to which we involved as accomplices those who did not even benefit from it.

History that repeats itself turns to farce. But a farce that repeats itself ends up making a history. This means that by repeating and doubling themselves up, even simulacra end up forming our material destiny—the only day of reckoning we have the right to now. (And maybe the only retrospective truth of history that, in this hypothesis, did not even wait to be repeated to become a farce.)

We can in this sense speak of the ephemeral, instable and reversible character of modernity (and of reality in general), and a different rate of universalization of rational values and the principle of reality that presides over them.

One should not believe that reality is equally distributed over the surface of the globe as if we were dealing with an objective world that was equal for everyone. Zones, entire continents have not seen the appearance of reality and its principle: they are underdeveloped in this generic sense that is more profound than the economic, technical or political. The West, after passing through a (historic) stage of reality, entered the (virtual) stage of ultra-reality. By contrast, a majority of the "rest of the world" have not even reached the stage of reality and (economic, political, etc.) rationality. Between the two, there are zones of reality, interstices, alveoli, shreds of reality that survive in the heart of globalization and the hyper-reality of networks—a bit like the shreds of territory that float to the surface of the map in Borgès' fable. One could speak of an index of reality, a rate of reality on the planet that could be mapped out like birthrates or the levels of atmospheric pollution. What would the maximum rate of reality be?

It remains to be seen whether this underdevelopment is a curse, if the non-access to the real and the rational is an absolute tragedy, or its contrary. One can ask this question when considering the advanced zones, the hyper-modern zones like our own that are already far from reality, that have lost its principle, that have devoured it in a way, in the space of two centuries, like any mineral fuel or natural deposit (moreover, the exhausting of reality goes hand in hand with the exhausting of natural resources). Hyper-real zones, still sub-lunar but already extraterrestrial, at once globalized and deterritorialized.

Opposition to global hegemony cannot be the same as opposition to traditional oppression. It can only be something unpredictable, irreducible to the preventive terror of programming, forced circulation, irreducible to the White terror of the world order. Something antagonistic, in the literal sense, that opens a hole in this Western agony. Something that leaves a trace in the monotony of the global order of terror. Something that reintroduces a form of impossible exchange in this generalized exchange. Hegemony is only broken by this type of event, by anything that irrupts as an unexchangeable singularity. A revolt, therefore, that targets systematic deregulation under the cover of forced conviviality, that targets the total organization of reality.

The high point of the struggle against domination was the historic movement of liberation, be it political, sexual or otherwise—a continuous movement, with guiding ideas and visible actors.

But liberation also occurred with exchanges and markets, which brings us to this terrifying paradox: all of the liberation fights against domination only paved the way for hegemony, the reign of general exchange—against which there is no possible revolution, since everything is already liberated.

Total revolt responds to total order, not just dialectical conflict. At this point, it is double or nothing: the system shatters and drags the universal away in its disintegration. It is vain to want to restore universal values from the debris of globalization. The dream of rediscovered universality (but did it ever exist?) that could put a stop to global hegemony, the dream of a reinvention of politics and democracy and, as for us, the dream of a Europe bearing an alternative model of civilization opposed to neoliberal hegemony— this dream is without hope. Once the mirror of universality is broken (which is like the mirror stage of our modernity), only fragments remain, scattered fragments. Globalization automatically entails, in the same movement, fragmentation and deepening discrimination—and our fate is for a universe that no longer has anything universal about it—fragmentary and fractal—but that no doubt leaves the field free for all singularities: the worst and the best, the most violent and the most poetic.

—*Montreal, October 2005*

3

WHERE GOOD GROWS

Marx: *Until now philosophers were content with interpreting the world. Now it has to be changed.*

Against Marx: *Today transforming the world is not enough. It will happen no matter what. What we urgently need today is to interpret this transformation—so that the world does not do it without us, and ends up being a world without us.*

The current revolution is different than previous historical revolutions—it is a truly anthropological revolution: a revolution in the automatic perfection of technical devices and in the definitive disqualification of human beings, of whom they are not even aware. At the hegemonic stage of technology, of world power, human beings have lost their freedom, but they have also lost their imagination. They have been made unemployed in a way that goes far beyond work: it is a mental and existential unemployment, replaced by dominant machines. These technical layoffs suggest the opposite of what the term usually means: the machines are not defective; they are so efficient that there is nothing left to do with one's life, whose very reproduction has become automatic. The obsolescence of humans has reached its terminal phase. Their fate is definitively beyond their reach. In the end, human beings will only have been an infantile illness of an integral technological reality that has become such a given that we are no longer aware of it, except in its transcendental dimensions of space and time.

This revolution is not economic or political. It is an anthropological and metaphysical one. And it is the final revolution—there is nothing beyond it. In a way, it is the end of history, although not in the sense of a dialectical surpassing, rather as the beginning of a world without humans. While history had a subject, there is no subject of the end of history. No more work of negative or historical finality...

It is the final stage of a world that we have given up interpreting, thinking or even imagining in favor of *implementing* it, instrumentalizing it objectively, or, better yet: launching ourselves into the unimaginable venture of performing it, turning into a performance, perfecting it—at which point it naturally casts us out.

This world no longer needs us. The best of all possible worlds no longer needs us.

Performance. Divestiture of humans and their freedom. Disqualification of humans in favor of automatism, a massive transfer of decision-making to computerized devices. A symbolic capitulation, a defeat of the will much more serious than any physical impairment. *Sacrifizio dell'intelletto, della voluntà, dell'immaginazione.*

Günther Anders gives a striking example of this divestiture during the Korean War. MacArthur wanted to use the atomic bomb, but the politicians took the decision away from him in favor of a battery of computers that calculated the "objective" benefits of the operation in political and economic terms—and that finally decided against using the bomb.

Nuclear conflict was avoided, but as G. Anders notes, symbolically, metaphysically, this abdication of human will, no matter what the consequences, for an impersonal concatenation, this *kidnapping* of human intelligence in favor of artificial intelligence was a far worse disaster than nuclear devastation. It marks the point where humans definitively renounced their destiny in favor of technological authority and its unquestionable superiority. It is not a transfer to a divine transcendence, or an adjustment of the will in favor of chance; it is a pure and simple capitulation of thought in the face of its technological double, reducing it to a voluntary servitude far more profound than the servitude of a people before their tyrant. The passage to electronic calculation, to engineering and computerizing is disastrous: more than a failure of the will, it implies the disappearance of every subject, be it the subject of power, knowledge or history, in favor of operational mechanics and the total deresponsibilization of humankind.

Today, power itself is an embarrassment and there is no one to assume it truly.

We can no longer match the perfection of our technological devices. What we produce is beyond our imagination and our representation. Humanity, confronted with its own divinized model, with the realization of its own ideal, collapses.

Our abilities, both in the domain of the imagination and responsibility and in the register of desire and pleasure, are completely surpassed. Those who believed in the unlimited morphological and anthropological adaptability of humankind and its ability to change at will were wrong.

Today, human beings have become the weak link in technological processes, in the *world-processing*.

The only choice left is between disappearing or being "humanengineerized." And the more the performance gap grows, the more human beings compensate for this failure by expanding their technological park, even extending it to Sloterdijk's "human park" and the biological modeling of the species. Ashamed of their incompleteness, humans have turned themselves into experimental beings.

We are, in our Promethean excesses, the only culture to have invented the perspective of ideal growth, of total performance, up to the supreme stage of reality. But we can no longer measure ourselves against this vertiginous dimension. Modernity (the West) can no longer respond to its own values of unlimited progress and growth.

Programming has transformed progress, which was an idea, a great historical idea, into a technological operation of the world in real time. And infinity, once an ideal abstraction, is materialized as well in infinite growth, the immediate vertigo of profusion.

And we are now prisoners of this irreversible dimension—unable to reinvent a finite universe.

Economic thinking has always wagered on infinite natural resources, on an incalculable horizon of material energies—the modern definition of energy being that it only demands to be "liberated" (the "liberation" of human beings and all of their faculties follows the same model).

With the threat of crises and the depletion of natural resources, economic thought has been touched by the grace of ecology and is rethinking its postulates on the possibility of infinite growth. But it is not rethinking the other postulate on the infinite availability of human beings to increasing amounts of happiness and pleasure. This anthropological illusion may be even more serious than the limits on resources. Humans are also limited in their potential. We imagine that needs, desires and demand are all endless and we have vigorously endeavored (especially since 1929) to convince them to respond with exponential demand to the exponentiality of growth. This is where the break comes in: humans break down. Their "libidinal and psychic resources" are drained. Although human beings can be exploited at will on the level of performance and production, on the level of aspirations and pleasure, they have limits. These limits draw an impassable line of resistance to the infernal machine of growth.

No one can stand this excrescence, this infinite proliferation—including the proliferation of the species with its six billion human beings.

Profusion is a kind of fatality—especially when people are overwhelmed, like the sorcerer's apprentice. They are not overcome by the malicious forces that they have unleashed, but by the best things they have created, the forces of Good that they have unleashed.

This paradoxical situation is not a contradiction between ends and means, between "science and morality," or a lack of balance between desire and the means to fulfill it. On the contrary, it is the hyperrealization of desire before it has even had time to appear that is the true curse.

It is not only happening on the individual and collective level, but on the level of the species as well. The entire species is passing through a moment of panic in the face of this overexposure to happiness and of this extravagant mastery of the world.

Starting with the irruption of reason, at the dawn of modernity, humankind launched itself on an escape trajectory outside itself, drawn beyond its possibilities. Space travel is only an extreme metaphor of this *takeoff*, this escape from mental territories.

This distortion, this excess leads to a growing depression, a decompensation, not from an inaccessible ideal, but from a form of excess gratification.

The rule of the game for the species, the symbolic rule of the game, is displaced.

The transformation is too fast for human beings to evolve and move from one form to another. We are losing the secret of all vital energy, which is never to go all the way, or to go beyond the possible. We are in the process of sacrificing this symbolic reserve of incompleteness in favor of a totalization of life through technology and a depletion of all desire. It is the "orgy." But what happens "*after the orgy*?" It becomes a schizo-phrenic farce, as Ceronetti said. Or rather the orgy turns into an ordeal, a judgment of God, decreeing that we are incapable of fulfilling our Promethean ambitions.

Socialization itself is in question. The present crisis, of which the disintegration of the *banlieues* is only the spectacular form, is the crisis of general disintegration in the face of the ideal demands of sociality. The disturbances in the margins conceal the fact that society as a whole is resisting the systematic colonization of socialization. The bar of total investment in life through society and economics has been set too high.

When did we discover that the deepest demands were social and economic, that the only horizon was the horizon of integration and calculation? Capital's *coup de force* is to make everything dependant on the economic order, to subject all minds to a single mental dimension. Every other issue becomes unintelligible. The displacement of all problems into economic and performance terms is a trap: the belief that everything is granted us virtually, or will be, by the grace of continual growth and acceleration—including, by extension, a universal lifting of prohibitions, the availability of all information and, of course, the obligation to experience *jouissance.*

Until now, everything was organized by the tension between desire and its fulfillment, between needs and their satisfaction. This critical situation was the source of all of our historical conflicts: protests, revolts, revolutions. Today, immediate consumption has moved far beyond the faculties of normal human beings to experience pleasure. Nothing tells us that people will now be able to bear insatiable desire after a millennium of shortages—nothing tells us that they are ready for total liberation. Nothing is less certain.

This is the true break, not a social fracture but a symbolic one: in the advent of an integral reality that absorbs all aspirations towards dreaming, surpassing or revolt.

> —*The despair of having everything.*
> —*The despair of being nothing.*
> —*The despair of being everybody.*
> —*The despair of being nobody.*

It is hard for us, with our reductive (economic and rational) anthropology, to imagine that being can shrink or revolt because it has been given too much. If lack and servitude characterized earlier societies, opulence and free markets characterize our society, which has entered its terminal phase and is ready for intensive care.

We are not succumbing to oppression or exploitation, but to profusion and unconditional care—to the power of those who make sovereign decisions about our well-being. From there, revolt has a different meaning: it no longer targets the forbidden, but permissiveness, tolerance, excessive transparency—the Empire of Good. For better or worse.

Now you must fight against everything that wants to help you.

New challenges, new context. However, the general atmosphere surrounding this new era, this new configuration is the obsolescence of humanity and its values.

—Obsolescence of Reason and the Enlightenment.
—Obsolescence of Universals and ideologies.
—Obsolescence of History and work.
—Obsolescence of desire and imagination.
—Obsolescence of the individual.

—Obsolescence of the Other.

—Obsolescence of reality.

—Obsolescence of death.

In fact, to describe this anthropological break, where all old values are obsolete and where all events take on another meaning, we would have to introduce the idea of a *non-Euclidean* space—the space of hegemonic world power, with its unprecedented machinery, but also the space of another type of events—events of another order than historical events—unpredictable events, without continuity or reference—and which are the radical sign of a counter-power at work.

The obsolescence of History opens a space where everything that was historical or political— including revolutions—has become "*fake*." All current political events, including the most violent ones, are made up of these *fake-events*, these *ghost-events*, which bear witness to a bygone history that is only the shadow of itself. In France, we see it today in melodramatic fashion. But the obsolescence of history and the political stage brings emerging events at the same time, events that I would call, by analogy with rogue states, *rogue events*—witnesses to the impossible revolution.

The only impossible revolution, says Ceronetti in substance, one that is even inconceivable to reason, would be the revolution against machines—

and this impossibility turns all other revolutions into a schizophrenic farce.

However, there are now traces of this impossible revolution in the (potentially terrorist) sequence of *rogue events* in the new non-Euclidean space.

Everything that was on the order of the negative and the work of the negative has now become parody—a counter-copy or transfer of the overall process. There is no return on that side. The critical threshold has been reached; there is no possibility of returning to Canetti's blind spot—no nostalgic transference of the situation. We are in a different space, the non-Euclidean space of power—a chaotic, stochastic, exponential, catastrophic and fractal universe of outsized effects (metalepsy), of the reversal of causality and reality.

BUT: if this non-Euclidean universe is now the universe of power, it has also become the universe of counter-power. This reversion is much more radical than a negation; the antagonism is capable of turning the weapons of this new power against it, and especially of turning the weapons of power against themselves.

The rules of hegemony are turned against it, through a force that contests it radically, in accordance with its own principles (and not only, like Marx in his time, according to historical contradictions while implicitly remaining faithful to the principle of reality and economic principles—to which his theory ends up succumbing).

That is why this is not a historical revolution but a kind of anthropological mutation, and while there is no revolution thinkable in the context of the current hegemonic power, there is nothing beyond this "non-Euclidean" counter-power.

An astounding illustration of this non-Euclidean space is September 11, which itself was an archetypal rogue event.

In the events of September 11, the most terrifying aspect was not the material destruction of the twin towers but the passage into something which, while inconceivable as reality (you can't believe your eyes, it's impossible), is not fiction at all. This fiction (from disaster movies, etc.) is part of our immune system; it protects us from reality by means of its double imaginary. It absorbs our fantasies. And the attack made our fantasies real—like a dream, like fulfilling a desire. Indeed, it was literally unlivable and the terror was there, in the inconceivable passage into reality—or rather in something that goes far beyond the real.

The real only exists to the extent that we can intervene in it. But when something emerges that we cannot change in any way, even with the imagination, something that escapes all representation, then it simply expels us.

In the collapse of the two towers, as opposed to the ordinary destruction of bombardment, where horizontal territory is struck from a vertical position, here the vertical dimension was struck head-on by the horizontal. A subversion of the usual orthogonal space—it is another topology—prefigured by the verticality of the towers, which was very different than the Empire State Building, for example.

The Empire State Building still represented the Promethean verticality of capital and wealth, of rivalry and domination. The Twin Towers, however, precisely because they were twins—which did not happen by chance—could only be measured against themselves: they mirrored each other in their self-referentiality. Their homotypy sealed the perfection of power that was no longer Promethean—I would call it Ouroborean, in the sense that it is enclosed in itself and defines a seamless (and windowless) hyperspace.

We can wonder what would have happened if only one of them fell. Impossible. The death of one could only lead to the death of the other, by symbolic contamination.

It was just as impossible to destroy them by a bomb in the basement, using the normal topology (the 1996 attack was a failure), for technical reasons, of course, but especially because they did not belong to that space (by analogy with hegemony, which cannot be fought in the traditional space of relationships of force and violence, because it no longer belongs to that space).

They had to be crashed into and made to implode (not explode) in their own space.

The masterstroke of the terrorists was to find a riposte beyond traditional confrontations, in this new extraterritorial dimension, a riposte equal to this new power. It is a new virtual power, in the sense in which it reigns and moves about in a space without reference, except to itself. An exponential power in the sense in which it is not measured by accumulation or ordinary verticality, but by an orbital structure that escapes determination "on the ground" and the constraints of reality.

This orbital and exorbitant form is the very form of hegemonic power and it can only be fought with other rules that come from radical alterity.

People were amazed by the poverty of the means used to obtain such a maximal result in this attack. But this new space is also the space of symbolic acts; it leads to chaotic, eccentric effects, effects with no common measure with the causes and effects of Euclidean space.

The extreme originality of this symbolic act was not only to pervert the most evolved technology by outflanking it, but to guess the possibilities of a different strategic space. It was no longer a head-on conflict—all frontal oppositions are caught despite themselves in a diabolic curve—but a true asymmetric conflict that implied, beyond relationships of force, a change in the rules of the game. A duel, with its oblique impact, that has all the characteristics of a martial art (of detour, of failure of the other and the diversion of its energy) and that is now traversing and destabilizing the entire political or geopolitical universe of globalization.

Every extension of hegemony is also an extension of terror. Let's be clear:

Beyond spectacular terrorism, terror should be seen as an infiltration, an internal convulsion, a form of power fighting itself. Power itself, from the inside, secretes an antagonistic power that materializes in one way or another—it could be Islam or it could be something else altogether. Every form is possible, but, for the most part, terror is a form of reversion—it is not necessarily violent, although in its most extreme form it necessarily implies death. The death of its victims, but first and foremost the death of the terrorists. September 11 put the spotlight on the symbolic use of death as an absolute weapon. The death of a terrorist is not a suicide: it is an effigy of the virtual death that the system inflicts on itself. From revolt to revolt, it takes multiple forms throughout history. From the sabotage and destruction of machines by Luddites in 1820 to Blacks burning their own neighborhoods in America in the 1960s, from general strikes to hostage taking and suicide attacks, we have gone increasingly farther into unilateral sacrifice, in suicidal violence without mercy or possible response—into the unexchangeable.

September 11-style terrorism has no truly objective causes or consequences—but it does have more profound ones. It is not a political event; it is a symbolic event. It does not give shape to a new world. It does not belong to the work of the negative, and therefore does not have a political destination.

We know that terrorism will not overthrow the world order. Its impact is much more subtle: a viral and elusive form that it shares with world power.

This is what makes the question of terror so complex: it is increasingly detached as a form from its visible actions and actors.

World power does not exactly need political power to ensure its hold. It exercises it in a very diffuse manner, through the mental diaspora of networks (which is why political actors and people in power are no longer part of it, even though they think they govern the world).

Terror does not exactly need terrorists now either. It is latent, infiltrating and virulent everywhere. It spreads in an endemic, interstitial, molecular state. All global culture is cannibalized by terror, by the discourse of terror. All information and media gravitate around it. The rest has become secondary. The global summit in Riyadh on combating terrorism rivaled the one in Davos on commerce or the one in Kyoto on global warming; same combat, same unanimity, all gimmicks, of course, but with no other alternative. Terrorism has become a *leitmotiv*, a universal focal point, a nebula—not a political or strategic reality, but a black hole, a blind spot.

Having infiltrated all of the networks of imagination and information, it might only exist as a specter. If, according to Marx, the specter of communism haunted Europe, today the specter of terror haunts the entire planet.

Even if there were no more living terrorists, the global psychosis would remain the same. In any case, Bin Laden does not need to be alive or to do anything; he only needs a phantom video from time to time. The system itself exploits the hyper-imagination of terror.

Terror is like a rumor: self-prophesying, self-realizing. Once it moves to the other side, and grows more violent than violence, it becomes an autonomous form without origin—like Evil itself.

It is irrepressible as well, because every form of "vigilance" aggravates the specter of terror. It is the paradox of every principle of precaution, and this principle has now been raised to the level of a global governing strategy. Security is quietly taking hold as a "white terror" draining the system of its Western values: freedom, democracy, human rights. This is the diabolical trap laid by the terrorists, forcing "democracies" to sabotage themselves "progressively."

A prime example of these rogue-events, which are both farcical and terrifying, is the recent bird flu scare (where the terrorists were wild ducks!).

There is no greater masquerade than this global panic, than the sacred union in panic. The international community becomes hectic and epileptic from the virus of terror and the terror of viruses. Terror is multiplied by the grotesque profusion of security measures that end up causing perverse autoimmune effects: the antibodies turn against the body and cause more damage than the virus. Without real solidarity between nations, the specter of Absolute Evil must be raised up as an *ersatz* Universal, an emergency solution to symbolic misery. When traditional contracts and symbolic pacts, the universal and the particular no longer function, a form like a conspiracy takes brutal shape, a plot in which everyone is involuntarily involved. Partaking in the conspiracy is not based on anything, on any value, other than delirious self-defense, in response to the total loss of the imaginary's immunity… In fact, the virus is a "*cosa mentale*" and contamination happens so quickly because the mental immunity, the symbolic defenses are long lost. A panic space can take hold in this liquidation, one to which the entire global information system also belongs for another reason, the system of networks and instant diffusion—a non-Euclidean space where all rational, preventive, prophylactic countermeasures are almost automatically turned against themselves through their own excesses. Security is the best medium for terror.

Yet we should also examine the conditions for the emergence of this virus and the sources of these new pathologies—not only in the animal world but in human society in general… One might guess that they are the result of confinement, promiscuity, concentration and monstrous overexploitation. The inevitable sequels of industrial processes. There is no difference between animal and human environments: the same conditions produce the same viral and infectious anomalies.

If we take for example the ingestion of bone meal leading to mad cow disease, there is a form of deregulation here, an incestuous confusion that it would be absurd to attempt to resolve by excess control and concentration-camp measures (the best solution found to fight the bird flu was sequestering animals and vaccinating migratory birds!).

Isn't the human species a carrier of countless germs and shouldn't it therefore be urgently "euthanized"?

And mad cow disease? Are we not, as the human species, like these poor mad cows? Aren't we being made to swallow, on every level, a strange bone meal—all of these ground-up messages, all of this meal of advertising and media production, this giant, milled junk heap of the news that we are stuffed with—like the meal made of bone, corpses and carcasses that we stuff our cows with—it is all bringing our species closer to spongiform encephalopathy.

The depths of terror are inseparable from the extension of farce. The terror of the Good much more than of Evil, which only follows like a shadow. The parody of the sacred union is taking hold everywhere, under the sign of a full preventive war against the slightest infectious molecule—but also against the least anomaly, the least exception, the least singularity.

The biting irony of this counter-terror, of white terror, is that it establishes a vast autoimmune syndrome, self-destruction through excess protection, which leads to crimes against humanity under the sign of the expulsion of Evil, crimes committed by humanity to get rid of itself completely, to cast itself out of an unlivable setting.

A few words now on these singular events and their curious sequences that do not follow historical continuity at all. We cannot speak of an "Axis of Evil" (the expression is absurd: there is only an Axis of Good), but we can speak of a convergence of different types of events with equivalent forms of terror. In recent years, after September 11, we have seen several examples: natural forces are confused with terrorist attacks as part of the same "Axis of Evil." Is it international terrorism that takes the shape of a natural disaster or is the tsunami the same as a terrorist attack? Bird flu, mad cow disease, atypical pneumonia, the blackout in New York, the heat wave are all abnormal events, all terrorist phenomena. The confusion is exploited in both directions: one group claims an accidental *crash* to be an attack, and another disguises an attack as an accident. Condoleezza Rice herself didn't hesitate in calling the tsunami a "wonderful opportunity" for a willing or coerced coalition of energies to fight the "forces of Evil." The dominant order itself forces us to have this unlimited conception of terrorism, since the slightest infraction, the slightest crime is denounced as a terrorist act. It comes as no surprise that natural disturbances have become an infraction against the world order.

The violence of natural disorders increases with the intensification of technological violence. Deregulation grows at the same rate as excesses in control and calculation. It is as if Nature were exacting revenge in the name of all of the peoples sacrificed and disowned. A symbolic backlash of insupportable hegemony, of the technological arraigning to which Nature responds in the "terrorist" form of earthquakes and eruptions. In the insurrection of natural elements, there is a hint of reprisal.

Evil is now everywhere and it must be eradicated. Every extreme phenomenon is Evil. It is the perfect alibi for the totalitarian extension of the Good. In a *New York Times* editorial cartoon (on bird flu): "*It's a pandemic. What should we do?*" Bush's response: "*Issue a terror alert!*" In this way we can understand how some in Islamic countries called on God to proclaim that the ravages of Hurricane Katrina were a terrorist act from the heavens striking the American sanctuary. A terrorist group could even lay claim to an earthquake. Because terror no longer belongs to anyone, no more than world power does. And because world power escapes everyone, it is now inscribed in things and in their objective unfolding.

One might object that major disasters (and particularly the most recent ones, the tsunami and Katrina) seem to favor the most disenfranchised populations—discriminating just as fiercely as globalization. It is true, but they also reveal this discrimination. They speak and reveal Evil.

Even the attack in Sharm el-Sheikh targeting international tourism is revelatory. We can understand how this universal tourism, bringing with it the general exchange of all cultures, the human equivalent of the flows of capital, the obnoxious infiltration and modern avatar of colonization and war, could be seen by the terrorists as an incarnation of all the values they abhor, as a viral infiltration— which is, in fact, what it is. Tourism itself is terrifying; it is a form of terror and can only attract terror in return.

A convection current of attacks and technological and natural disasters has formed carrying a touch of Evil—the smallest accidents now take the symbolic turn of a secret counter-finality.

Just as networks connect all points on the globe and all markets in real time through universal electronic interactions, events enter a network or follow each other in a symbolic hyperspace, no matter what their nature. Attacks, disasters, accidents and epidemics all go in the same direction, towards a dismantling of the global order. And they can join in a chain reaction because their objective causes are indifferent or marginal and they seem to obey an internal logic: their own escalation. They are hyper-sensitive to each other and signal each other beyond the normal flow of news.

World power eludes everyone because it is no longer the effect of a dominating will but of an automatic and irreversible mechanism. As a result, the mechanism of disaggregation of this power also escapes everyone and cannot be stopped. This system should worry much less about revolution than about what is developing in the void, at the heart of the anthropological fracture.

The more intense this hegemonic process of forced integration and integral reality is, the more singularities will rise against it. There will be more "rogue states"—states (like Iran, Palestine) that deliberately exclude themselves from the international community without waiting to be excluded, that exclude themselves from the universal and play their own game, at their own risk and peril. There will be more "rogue events" and more refusal of society by individuals.

One could say, inverting Hölderlin, that "Where Good grows, there grows the Genie of Evil," ("*Da, wo des Gute wächst, wächst auch der Genius des Bösen*"). This more or less clandestine insurrection of antagonistic forces against the integrist violence of the system is less an effect of the mind, the will or even the desire of human beings than the evil genius of the world itself in refusing globalization.

To find the only adversary who will face this all-powerful hegemony, we must look for those beings that are strangers to will, exiled from dialogue and representation, exiled from knowledge and history.

We must look for the "less-dead-than-us."

This expression comes from the astounding statement by Philippe Muray addressing jihadists after September 11. He thought that the game was played out and that this terrorism had no future. And he told them, in the name of the West: "We will defeat you because we are deader than you."

This expression assumes that some people in the world are less dead than others, that others in the world are less dead than us (the West). The hypothesis remains that if the West is dead, there must exist (even in the West) an opposing power with a singularity, in all its forms, that counterbalances this hegemonic power. Against the empire of Good, a spark of Evil.

The "less-dead-than-us" belong to those who are on the other side of the symbolic wall, the wall that separates the two worlds throughout the planet—the equatorial line of a new violence that we can see in the images of barbed wire in Melilla, the wall on the US-Mexican border or the one in Israel—the wall that contains and provokes a human wave, a backlash of discrimination.

The Universal is not for everyone. Only discrimination is universal.

In the past, totalitarian powers were the ones who enclosed themselves behind walls (the best historical example being the Berlin Wall) to escape the wave of "democracy." Now these "democracies" are building protective walls to preserve the correct use of freedom from the hordes of immigrants or fanatics. If oppression was only possible behind the Soviet Iron Wall, today, freedom is only possible behind the iron wall of democracy.

However, we can be sure that any wall—even a transparent one—is the sign of a dictatorship or a totalitarian system. We must therefore recognize that the West has become a totalitarian space—the space of a self-defensive hegemony defending itself against its own weakness. A wall is always suicidal: as soon as communism raised the Berlin Wall, it was virtually lost. It could only crumble in the end like the wall that it erected against itself.

The same is true of the Israelis and their security fence. Any protection only leaves the field open for deadly impulses from the inside.

But this exodus to the Western world through the wall of discrimination is also a cannibalistic infiltration that passes through all barriers that oppose it. In any case, even in the West, we are all already virtually exiled, extradited, expulsed, filtered out.

If nothing else can justify the violence carried out in the name of the Universal except the idea that everyone can one day have access to it, then we must admit that the vast majority will never reach it, and that we, the civilized nations of the West, are far off the mark. Take as evidence the disturbances caused by all of the "rogue events" that have taken place here. These "transpolitical" events should not be interpreted in economic or political terms, which would return them to the nothingness of the political scene and its ridiculousness. We should interpret them as symptoms of the schizophrenic farce now being played out.

April 21, 2002, the "No" vote on the European referendum, the riots in the suburbs and the social movement against the CPE (first employment contract). Confronted with their own objectives (when they exist), they are insignificant—the zero degree of an impossible revolution. But if we interpret them on a global level, in the framework of this global antagonism, then they become "micro rogue-events," an almost instinctive abre-action, no matter what their ideology, to the deregulatory machine of world power.

In some ways, the "No" on the referendum, the illogical and unexplainable "No," or the revolts in the suburbs come from the same demand. It is not a demand to be "integrated." On the contrary, it is a demand not to be integrated at all, or tethered or annexed or taken hostage by any model (especially an ideal one!), because it always hides an absolutely deadly totalitarian arrangement, an unquestioned fundamentalism. And in this sense, maybe they are "less-dead-than-others."

Wherever this global confrontation will lead, nothing is yet decided and the suspense remains total.

4

THE ROOTS OF EVIL

Chronic'art: *In recent years, your texts have developed a new central idea, the idea of Evil and more precisely absolute Evil. What is this absolute Evil? What does it represent? What is its place in our society today?*

Jean Baudrillard: The notion of Evil is always very ambiguous. I would distinguish between at least two versions of Evil. There is relative Evil, which is Evil as it is generally understood. This Evil only exists in balance with Good, in equilibrium and permanent opposition with Good. But now there is also an absolute Evil, a depressive or catastrophic version of this relative Evil. There is no longer any sharing or antagonism here between Good and Evil. This absolute Evil comes from an excess of Good, an unchecked proliferation of Good, of technological development, of infinite progress, of totalitarian morality, of a radical will to do good without opposition. This Good turns into its opposite, absolute Evil. Traditionally, relative Evil was only in opposition; it did not have its own essence or root and therefore, in particular, it did not have its own finality. In contrast, this absolute Evil has a finality: as Good, it has an ideal finality— to do good—but this ideal finality turns catastrophic, and turns into absolute Evil. It is an absolute, irreparable, inexorable movement. We find here again the idea of reversibility. Ordinarily, this is a dynamic vector, but in this tautological operation, Good turning catastrophic has severe consequences. In our discourse, Evil is just a mask that we contrast with the Good that we are supposed to defend. The key concept is the "Axis of Evil." This axis was discovered as a malevolent incantation, and not only a moral rite this time. It may even be an obscure awareness of the unhappy destiny of the enterprise of Good. It is a type of exorcism, with the foreboding that Good is doomed, but also, beyond this unconscious, automatic and convulsive projection, it is a strategy consisting of projecting Evil everywhere, obviously as a perfect alibi for doing Good. One positions an Axis of Evil where there is none. Good is directive, directional; it has a finality in principle and therefore constitutes an axis. Evil is more of a parallax. It is never directional, and is not even opposed to Good. There is always some kind of diversion, a deviation, a curve. As Good goes straight ahead, Evil deviates. It is a deviance, a perversion. You never know where Evil is going, or how. It cannot be mastered. In almost topological terms, it is merely a deviation. Only Good could lay claim to being an axis. But this axis is projected on Evil; an imaginary Axis of Evil is created to justify the Axis of Good. This is a strategic mistake. When you try to target Evil in its unfindable axis, when you fight it militarily, with a frontal attack, you can only miss it.

Because this Axis of Evil is within the order of discourse. It only exists in the mouths of Western leaders and serves as self-legitimization: the ones who speak about the Axis of Evil need to show that they work for Good and for everyone's happiness in order to exist. No individual fights in the name of Evil.

Of course. To a certain extent, the imputation of Evil always comes from the Good, from the sanctuary that, in principle, houses the rules of the game, the law, the truth. But Evil is indefinable, and therein lies its power. Yet through a twisting or retaliation of Evil against Good, those who defend Good feel themselves obliged to define this indefinable Evil. It is not a Manichean position—I prefer Manichaeism—because Good and Evil are not playing the same game. On the one side, there is the Good, which has sole claim to the truth effect, the reality effect. On the other, Evil causes a crack in this identification, which disrupts the automatic writing of the world by Good. In the name of Good, people try to give shape to Evil, for example in the terrorism that they see everywhere. In the discourse of Good, terrorism and Evil become one and the same thing, to such an extent that nature, just like fundamentalism, can be seen as a terrorist. Terror takes shape. But it is the shape of a delusion. The era of terror is not the irruption of an Evil that was waiting for its time to come. I may be naïve or cynical, but I do not see Evil as an identifiable axis embodied by men or organizations to be fought, but as an irrepressible drive for revenge on the excesses of Good. It is a wild and deviant revenge against an unacceptable state of things, vengeance, a retaliation that exercises and expresses a violent necessity for rebalancing, at least symbolically.

Can we say that in order to exist and develop, these forces of Good have taken so much power, had such an impact on the entire world, created such disequilibrium, that Evil appears, or explodes on the planet like a time bomb?

We live in a virtually banalized, neutralized world where, because of a kind of preventive terror, nothing can take place any longer. Therefore everything that breaks through is an event. The definition of an event is not to be unpredictable but to be pre-destined. It is an irrepressible movement: at one moment, it comes out, and we see the resurgence of everything that was plotted by the Good. It makes a break, it creates an event. It can be on the order of thought or of history. It may take place in art. And, of course, it assumes the form of what is called terrorism. But, again, it is not a frontal opposition, but more like a reversal in the heart of Good. The event comes from Good, not from Evil, and in it Good turns into its opposite. By taking the curvature of Evil, Good is degraded; it decomposes, it self-destructs. Global power, the power of the West—more than just the United States, which is its archetype—has no symbolic response to terrorism because terrorism wagers its own death in its acts of suicidal destruction. Global power cannot respond to this desire for death by wagering its own death. It responds through physical, military extermination in the name of Good against the Axis of Evil. Global power has no symbolic response because it consists of awesome symbolic power-lessness. For about a century, the West has worked at the degradation of its own values, eliminating and abolishing them. Abolishing everything that gives value to something, someone or a culture. Simulation and simulacra participate in this phe-nomenon. This process of abjection, humiliation, shame, self-denial, this fantastic masquerade has become the strategy of the West and is amplified by the United States. The West, having destroyed its own values, finds itself back at the zero degree of symbolic power, and in a turnabout, it wants to impose the zero degree on everyone. It challenges the rest of the world to annihilate itself symbolically as well. It demands that the rest of the world enter into its game, participate in the generalized, planetary exchange and fall into its trap. Then an extraordinary potlatch comes into play between global power and the powers opposing it, between those who wager their own death and those who cannot wager it because they no longer control it. The game does not end there. There is a moral and philosophical confrontation, almost a metaphysical one, beyond Good and Evil. Islam? The United States? It doesn't matter! There is a confrontation between two powers. It is an asymmetrical potlatch between terrorism and global power, and each side fights with its own weapons. Terrorism wagers the death of terrorists, which is a gesture with tremendous symbolic power and the West responds with its complete powerlessness. But this powerlessness is also a challenge. Challenge versus challenge. When people make fun of the carnival, the masquerade of the elections in America every four years, they are being too hasty. In the name of critical thought, of very European, very French thought, we do a contemptuous analysis of this kind of parody and self-denial. But we are wrong, because the empire of simulation, of simulacra, of parody, but also of networks, constitutes the true global power. It is more founded on this than on economic control. The essential is in the extraordinary trap set for the rest of the world so that everyone goes to the zero degree of value, a trap that fascinates the rest of the world.

In this light, the story of the Italian hostage in Iraq was a fascinating one. When the Italian secret services agent that freed her from the terrorists was killed by US soldiers, it was Good assassinating Good, Good doing Evil in the name of Good. It was a total confusion of the two, where we could see how the Empire of Good is also an Empire of Evil, because it self-destructs. Such is the fatal destiny and the curse of the Empire of Good when it wants to finish its work. This story was a concrete example, and a very enlightening one. We know that everything that reaches its absolute end is reversed. That is exactly what happened. The American soldiers finished the work. Today, there are many stories like that one, and we could compile a black book with all of these reversals of things.

Finding Evil on your own side because it is no longer identifiable elsewhere, is that the ultimate stage of self-destruction?

I often speak of "cannibalization": power cannibalizes itself in the sense that it devours itself. I also think of it in terms of "cannibalizing" a car or selling it for spare parts. The car cannot be used as a car, but you can do something with the parts. A culture can be cannibalized in the same way, with the negotiation and sale of its values as spare parts. But the whole will never work again.

The attraction of the empire of simulation, the world's desire to live in such a masquerade, the aspiration for the void but also the empire's will to extend its domain over the entire planet, are they the new forms of domination?

We must distinguish between domination and hegemony. Until now, we were dealing with domination, a master/slave relationship, a symbolic one if you like, a dual relationship with the possibility of explosion, revolution, alienation and disalienation. This domination has made way for hegemony, which is something else altogether. There is no longer a dual relationship. Everyone is an accomplice. And hegemony uses this complicity to lower individuals even more, playing on everyone's desire to lower themselves in this way. Hegemony works by devaluing everyone. There are no longer dominants and dominated, but a kind of total annexation (*nexus* = networks). Everyone is caught up in the network and submits to this hegemony. Who benefits? We can no longer calculate in terms of benefits for one power or another. We can no longer go back in history to find out who is responsible for the domination. We are both victims and accomplices, guilty and not responsible. Hegemony is within us. It is the next phase of domination. I think it is worse, because hegemony brings domination, and therefore alienation, to an end. We are no longer alienated; alienation is no longer the problem. And yet we suffer. We have fallen into an irreversible vertigo; we are drawn to the black hole. We can sense the strategy but there is no one behind it. The black hole is what I call integral reality. And this integral reality, the signature of this new hegemony, is frightening because we cannot resist it. If we want to resist hegemony and escape it using the means we once used against domination (revolt, critical thought, negative thought, etc.), there is no hope.

In a text published earlier this year in Libération *("Rebonds," February 17, 2005) you mention the Holocaust and the tsunami as new examples of this Evil that the forces of Good must stigmatize as Evil in order to exist. Is this part of the same logic?*

The tsunami and the reactions it elicited throughout the world were the starting point for my text; the Holocaust came in later. The Empire of Good found a great opportunity in the December 2004 tsunami to do good in the eyes of the world, to expand Good and extend its empire. In doing so, it found Evil in a place where, in principle, according to rational thought, it should not and should never be: a natural disaster. It may seem like an archaic projection to think that natural disasters are Evil, although from the point of view of the global order, it is completely justifiable to fight them as a form of terrorism. In this text for *Libération*, I said that God himself had become a terrorist. Nothing can now be seen outside of this light.

And what is the relationship to the Holocaust commemorations?

The Holocaust connection is a little more complicated, but it participates in the same syndrome. The idea of making the Holocaust into such an absolute reference point and no longer taking it as what it is, as a tragic historical event with antecedents and consequences, a possibility of analysis... After the 50th anniversary in 1995, the 60th anniversary of the Holocaust was commemorated. Between the two, I noticed disparities and a change of perspective: all at once, this tragic event was transformed into a mythology. It had already begun, but it became visible and global at that point. Everyone was concerned, including countries and cultures that had nothing to do with it. It was truly the elaboration of an alibi. Moreover, if you do not assert that the Holocaust is the absolute crime, you are immediately on the side of Evil. I know what I'm talking about, because I am not a stranger to this type of accusation. Ten years ago, no one was trying to transform it into a global myth by mythifying and therefore mystifying it. This transformation of event into myth evacuates the question of Evil all the more in that it perpetuates the confusion between Evil and misfortune [*Mal* and *malheur*]. The Holocaust is Evil. Yet it is possible, even desirable, to have an intelligence of this Evil, but not if we confuse the Holocaust and *malheur*. If we do, it can be negotiated like any value, it becomes the object of pathos that is much stronger because the misfortune is absolute. This misfortune is shared and can only be shared in its most pathetic form. To be happy or unhappy implies a pathetic affect. Evil has nothing to do with affect. It is beyond morality, beyond judgment. To an astounding degree, the commemoration confronted us with this pathetic "image replay" of absolute, disconsolate misfortune. The problem is that by making a historical event into absolute misfortune, there is no room left to distance ourselves and to gain any intelligence of Evil.

Is this the first time that we have seen the mythification of an event?

No, of course not. There have been operations like this in every culture. But it so happens that our culture is based precisely on the mastery of these operations, and this is a dangerous relapse. When someone like Dieudonné calls this commemoration "memorial pornography," he is completely right. But people make it sound like he is saying that the Holocaust is pornographic, and that amalgam does not work. But it is the amalgam made by the media that is scandalous. I say the same thing, in a different way. Is it more subtle? I don't know.

Especially since it is you, Jean Baudrillard, who is saying it.

Yes. But I did not get any response from the article that appeared in *Libération*. Everyone stayed quiet. What should I do, cause a scandal? That is not my style. It would just prolong a pointless controversy.

But there is something very powerful behind the new myth and the absolute misfortune that are confused with Evil. Isn't this confusion between the two intentional?

We are supposed to be able to fight misfortune, and we even attempt to theorize it subjectively today: rampant victimality at every level and recriminations. We are in misfortune; we acknowledge it and enact it. The exact same thing happens with misfortune as with Western culture enacting its own degradation. The identity reflex is found in misfortune itself. Which brings us back to hegemony. In a system of domination, when you are a slave or even a salaried worker, you are in any case on the losing side, but you exist as such and not as a victim. And that is why you can go on strike or revolt. In a hegemonic regime, on the contrary, we are not slaves but hostages. We are therefore all victims, all in misfortune. In Greek, the word "hegemon" signifies the person who governs, who leads; it is governance and therefore has the same meaning as "cyber," which etymologically means the "art of piloting" or "governing." The era of hegemony is the era of the cyber system. It governs, it regulates, but it does not dominate. There are no longer any exploited or dominated. There is something else, something much harder to overtake by surprise. It is harder to critique as well, because critical thought is devitalized in this case. It is absorbed, like a victim condemned to expressing him- or herself in the void, or to emptying him- or herself of all substance. There is the impression that History is no longer driven by development but by an indeterminate and uncontrollable growth. An invasion has taken place. It is like a turbo: it is a turbo-system drawn by the vacuum that it creates before it. Something really happened in the last five or ten years, between the two commemorations of the Holocaust. September 11 occurred and started a mutation. Not in terms of political, economic or strategic consequences, but there was a phase inversion in the system. September 11 was a pre-destined event. It would not have had the same resonance if it had not concretized or symbolically materialized something that had been real for a long time: this loss of value in a self-devouring, cannibalistic culture. No one realized it, it could have gone on indefinitely, but then, suddenly, the image froze. Inside this disintegrating power, at least virtually threatened by itself, something was violently materialized before the eyes of the entire world. This is the very definition of an event: when an illegible, long-running process becomes legible at a given moment by the force of an unprecedented act.

You mention clones several times in Cool Memories V. *What does this figure represent in the Empire of Good as you describe it?*

Clones are the possibility of perpetuating the species artificially. The question is whether we attach a strong symbolic value to the human species as such. If so, then clones are deviant, perverted. They negate the symbolic dimension of a species that implies the disappearance of each individual to continue to evolve. But here, people are seeking immortality. They do not want to disappear; they want to make the disappearance disappear! What they do not want to see, however, is that this desire for cloning is just another way of disappearing, and a shameful one. It is a technological disappearance into artificial survival, corresponding to the elimination of the human as human. And this process of disappearance has already begun.

Does this objective bother you morally?

Ethically, I am against it. But I am against ethical positions in general. Let us say that I oppose it in symbolic terms.

For you, clones, like integral reality, are an image of the absolute perfection that is presented as a desirable perfection, while they are only something else, like an acceptable name for the death of the species.

If you attempt to bring an end to sexuality and death, what rules are you contravening? Laws, they do not interest me, but symbolic rules? What happens if you eliminate the truth that all singularities imply their own disappearance? You appear, you disappear. If you eliminate disappearance, there is no more singularity. And that seems to be the only thing that can resist, that cannot be reduced to the integral, total, totalitarian hold of insurmountable reality. With clones, this singularity explodes. You could call it progress; it all depends on the point of view. Clones are just one example among others. I also include the "ordination," "computerization" and digitalization of the world in this process.

Artificial intelligence as well?

Yes. I was recently reading a praise of plants and vegetation that offered a surprising point of view: what distinguishes animals from plants is sexuality and death, because plants are immortal in a certain way due to their method of reproduction by scissiparity. In our advanced, scientific and technological culture, we are taking the path of plants. We are becoming vegetal. Using our technology, we are trying to neutralize sexuality (including by generalizing it) and neutralize death. We are entering the system of unlimited metastasis of the plant. Networks, the Internet and all of these things are unlimited metastasis!

Reading the text, I found it funny to see how we may be deteriorating, passing from the animal to the plant stage, and God knows where it will end. Why plants after all? It could be very good, for better or worse. I admire trees. I am not praising the plant stage, but there is an anthropological mutation if not an ontological one. Where are Good and Evil in this context? The question of Good and Evil is not asked here. There is a mutation, that much is clear. The right question is therefore: how far will we go? Will we go back to the almost inorganic state of the protozoa? This can already be found in Freud with the death drive. Is that what is involved here? Or is there a propulsive momentum leading us to another form of disappearance, because in any case we will disappear? But we will disappear in a kind of illumination and not symbolically.

You say that artificial intelligence is both the death of intelligence and the death of consciousness. Is that what we reject in the machine, both intelligence and consciousness?

Artificial intelligence is the reign of hegemony. The brain has become the biological version of hegemony; everything is subordinated to the brain, as the image of order, of the computer. Everything is governed, cybernetized, brought back to the ordering power of the brain. Everything else, the body, is left aside. Other cultures disdained the brain. For the Greeks, it did not even exist; it was useless viscera. For us, the brain rules with a form of digital, binary intelligence in this case that is not at all the same thing. As for consciousness, what place would it have in this digital universe? It is a form of intelligence, but it does not think, as Heidegger would say, it calculates. It is a positive intelligence. The negative is completely left out again. There is no work of the negative here.

In the cybernetic universe where everything is calculable, can't Evil in the sense of disorder and chaos slip into and penetrate the integral reality of the network? Isn't that what hackers do for example?

Accidents are involved, certainly. Paul Virilio speaks of this much better than I can. But what I am saying is of another order: it is unpredictable. It is power turning against itself. It is not necessarily the apocalypse but it is a disaster in the sense of a form made irrepressible regardless of the will of the actors and their negative actions or sabotage. Certainly, many negative things can happen to the system, but it will always be an objective or objectal negativity related to the technology itself, not a symbolic irruption. I am afraid that this game remains internal to integral reality. Perhaps there are some who can penetrate the cracks in this cybernetic universe? I must say that I do not know the internal rules of the game for this world, and I do not have the means to play it. This is not a philosophical or moral disavowal or prejudice on my part. It is just that I am situated somewhere else and I cannot do otherwise. From the outside, I can see that everything works and that the machine allows everything to function. Let us allow that system to proceed normally—or abnormally— until it runs its course; let us leave to the machine what belongs to the machine without trying to humanize it or make it an anthropoid object. For me, I will always have an empty, perfectly non-functional and therefore free space where I can express my thoughts. Once the machine has exhausted all of its functions, I slip into what is left, without trying to judge or condemn it. Judgment is foreign to the radicality of thought. This thinking has nothing scientific, analytic or even critical about it, since those aspects are now all regulated by machines. And maybe a new space-time domain for thought is now opening?

semiotext(e) intervention series

☐ 1: The Invisible Committee: The Coming Insurrection
☐ 2: Christian Marazzi: The Violence of Financial Capitalism
☐ 3: Guy Hocquenghem: The Screwball Asses
☐ 4: Tiqqun: Introduction to Civil War
☐ 5: Gerald Raunig: A Thousand Machines
☐ 6: Jean Baudrillard: The Agony of Power
☐ 7: Tiqqun: This Is Not a Program
☐ 8: Chris Kraus: Where Art Belongs